T0266086

PAGES FROM A SCRAPBOOK OF IMMIGRANTS

The Photograph

He finds it in his mother's drawer of souvenirs,
blurred and bent: an out-of-focus photograph
as brown and cracked as leather.
The trees and foliage arch like feathers.
There is a house, one story, in the rear,
behind the lumpy humans growing up—
those arms and shoulders so rigidly posed,
those faces like smudged thumbprints on a wall.
He must recognize these children—
by a slouch, a shape, a tilt of the head—
as his uncles and aunts. One daughter
is massive, and the other, the boy's mother,
is as slim and tall as her eldest brother
and the man who sits stiff-backed in front
beside the round little woman in a shawl.

The details of each shape are so off-center,
the photo looks as if it had been taken
at the instant people, house, and trees
were shaken by an earthquake or a wind.
The more he looks at it, the more the boy
cannot be sure of where this is, or when.
The house could be in Kovno, Vilna, or Carnarsie.
Is this his uncle, really? That his aunt?
The photo could belong to someone else.
The family could be anyone's.

OTHER BOOKS BY MORTON MARCUS:

Poetry

Origins (Kayak, 1969; third edition, 1974)
There the Oceans Cover Us (Capra Press, 1972)
The Santa Cruz Mountain Poems (Capra Press, 1972)
The Armies Encamped in the Fields beyond the Unfinished Avenues
    (Jazz Press, 1977; Brown Bear Reprints edition, 1988)
Big Winds, Glass Mornings, Shadows Cast by Stars (Jazz Press, 1981;
    second edition, 1984; Brown Bear Reprints edition, 1988)

Fiction

The Brezhnev Memo (Dell Books, 1980)

PAGES FROM
A SCRAPBOOK OF IMMIGRANTS

A JOURNEY IN POEMS BY MORTON MARCUS

COFFEE HOUSE PRESS :: MINNEAPOLIS :: 1988

The author wishes to thank the following publications where many of these poems first appeared: *Poetry* (Chicago), *Ironwood, TriQuarterly, Poetry Northwest, Reaper, Quilt #4, Poetry Now, Ally, The Porter Gulch Review, Quarry West, Cream City Review, Margin, Hubbub,* and ZYZZYVA. "The Wolf without His Teeth" appeared in *Poetry* (Chicago). "The Immigrant" appeared as a broadside from Moving Parts Press, and was sponsored by George Ow, Jr. "A Great-Uncle Remembers his Phantom Horses" and "Dinner At Grandpa's" appeared in *The Anthology of Magazine Verse & Yearbook of American Poetry*, 1985 and 1986/87 respectively.

My thanks to Sue Bergholz for her enthusiasm for the book and her unending energy in placing it with a publisher, and to Jack Marshall, Tim Sheehan, Joe Stroud, and David Swanger for their excellent suggestions on early versions of the manuscript.

My special thanks to Fred Levy, Kirby Wilkins, and Al Young who, in the midst of hectic lives, suggested important revisions after detailed readings of the finished work.

This project is supported in part by: The National Endowment for the Arts, a federal agency, Star Tribune/Cowles Media Company, and United Arts. The publishers also thank Minnesota Center for Book Arts, where Coffee House has been a Visiting Press since 1985.

Coffee House Press books are available to bookstores through our primary distributor: Consortium Book Sales and Distribution, 213 East Fourth Street, Saint Paul, Minnesota 55101. Our books are also available through all major library distributors and jobbers, and through most small press distributors, including Bookpeople, Bookslinger, Inland, Pacific Pipeline, and Small Press Distribution. For personal orders, catalogs or other information, write to: Coffee House Press, Post Office Box 10870, Minneapolis, Minnesota 55458.

Library of Congress Cataloging in Publication Data

Marcus, Morton.
     Pages from a scrapbook of immigrants: a journey in poems / by Morton Marcus.
          p.   cm.
     ISBN 0-918273-47-1 (alk. paper) : $8.95
     1. Russian Americans—Poetry.   I. Title.
PS3563.A639P3   1988
     811'.54—dc19   88-30234
                                   CIP

Contents

The Photograph

This book

is for all our families

PART 1

THE OLD WORLD

My mission on earth is to recognize the void—inside and outside me—and fill it.

—MENAHEM-MENDEL OF VITEBSK

Literature is the memory of humanity.

—ISAAC BASHEVIS SINGER

THE OLD COUNTRY

There is snow outside,
or yellow wheat, miles of it.
The towns are islands
in a sea of wheat, wooden islands
that crack and creak.
The sun broils down, or the wind
sharpens its sting against the house,
and you are sure that relatives
in towns a hundred miles away or more
broil or shiver just like you.
Peasants here
drive in from the fields
and one day bargain with you
in the market square, the next
grab at your women, beat your children
or snip their earlocks for a joke,
or shave off half your beard.
Cossacks swagger through the streets
and gallop their horses
at any Jewish gesture in the road.
Beyond these townships
are the Czar, St. Petersburg, and Minsk.
And watching over all is God,
who, His people understand,
must wait for that moment
he has inlaid somewhere ahead
in the elaborate dark
to rescue them.

GRATITUDE

A Folk Tale

Wanting to say "Thank you," the husband merely nods.
When she hangs up his cloak, refills his tea glass,
an obstruction enters his throat,
as if turning a corner on a mountain path
he encounters a boulder among fallen rock.
He can pray, kiss the knuckles of the barmaid
serving vodka, call, "Thank you! Thank you!"
in the wake of dust from the landowner's carriage,
weep in gratitude for another son
beneath the inky dome of the star-splotched sky,
but when she hands him his caftan or serves him soup,
the boulder blocks his path.

He asks three of his brothers for help,
then three neighbors, then three men
he drinks with in the tavern, men whose origins
are never clear. But each time,
the others stand behind him, caps in hand,
heads bowed, and do not say a word,
as if the flat hot landscape with its miles of wheat
has stunned them to silence. And so they stand,
like mountains that the wife just stares at
from the porch. And so they remain,
a range of mountains to the west
that loom before her every morning
and attend the silence of her days
as, daily, her husband goes about his chores.

His silence becomes her life. She makes beds with it,
mops with it, raises gardens from it,
cooks with it, and feeds her four daughters on it—
those same daughters who grow up solemn-eyed
and like their mother spend each day
among furniture and cooking pots, muttering complaints
of backache and drafts and intestinal inflammation.

Three of the men these girls will marry
have big hands and small voices:
two are farmers, one a carpenter. The fourth
is a small, round, nearsighted tailor
who always nods and seems to address
the clothes of the person he is talking with.

When a marriage contract is agreed upon,
the matchmaker brings the fiancé to visit.
And so the first three men come, caps in hand, and sit.
They drink tea and sit. They clear their throats and sit.
They look out the window at the mountains and sit.
The daughters sit, too, and shift in their crinolines.
Oh, the first three betrothal visits aren't on the same day,
but they might as well be.

                        The tailor is the last to come.
Seated in a suit his plump white hands have sewn,
he wags his head inside a stiff white collar.
The mother hands him tea, a glass of it with a spoon inside.
He nods, smiles, and looks at the stitching on her cuff.
"Thank you," he whispers to the shawl across her shoulders,
"thank you" to the lace collar beneath it on her dress.
The father slaps his knees and jumps to his feet.
"THANK YOU!" he roars. "THANK YOU! THANK YOU!"
and raises triumphant fists above his head.
Next he bites his mustache and dances for an hour,
a boot-slapping dance that rattles the floor
and makes the matchmaker and his yellow-haired daughter
lean together tittering and trembling.
Then he whirls the wide-eyed tailor around the room,
until his wife reaches toward him from her chair—
smiling now where she had wept an hour before—
and the old man sets the tailor down, falls at her feet,
and mutters, "Thank you! Thank you!" again and again
as he beats his head on her knees.

A GREAT-GREAT-UNCLE'S STORY

*In 1827 Czar Nicholas I decreed that when Jewish males
reached the age of eighteen, they were to be conscripted into the
Russian army for twenty-five years. He soon lowered the age to
twelve, so the children could be more easily Russianized, while
his officers stole boys younger than that off village streets . . .*

He is eight, so they throw him in line
and surround him with an overcoat
that shows he is a soldier now.
His mother shrieks and moans.
Twenty-five years he will serve,
and then come back, a man of thirty-three—
here marching off with other boys
through crusty mud and ice-edged winds
to God knows where.

                    Most of the boys
do not make it to the training camp,
and those who do live on *traife* and biscuits
and get kicked and pulled by the ear
until they kiss the icon or the cross
and swear by the false messiah's holy name.
Some crumple up in corners, refuse to eat,
and, staring, die.
Others just cough themselves into the grave.

But he comes back at thirty-three,
and the way he swaggers through the streets,
as lean and flexible as a leather whip—
well, he seems more Russian now
than Jewish. He marries
and has several sons, but the neighbors
keep their distance.

They know how he has suffered
and how his family has prayed,

but to see him toss a vodka back
or grin like any peasant
or to observe his ease
around the cossacks and the cops
bewilders them, makes them shudder.

A rumor goes around
that for all those years
he'd eaten pork. He never denies it.
He smokes his pipe in front of the house,
stares over rooftops, and tells his sons
that there are things far worse
than *traife*. But he never elaborates,
and the boys grow up despising this man
whom the Russians greet as one of their own.

His neighbors grumble. It isn't his fault,
everyone agrees. They just feel
that there's something unnatural in him
and shake their heads. But their children
deride his children, call them unclean,
hit them with sticks, and although he must know,
he never complains.

            At his funeral
a Russian sergeant stands in uniform.
All the Jews admit they are impressed
and remember that this uncle
won medals during the Crimean War.
But the sergeant, it turns out,
young and fidgety in his high stiff collar,
has been assigned to come
and only knows the dead one's name.

A Great-Uncle Remembers His Phantom Horses

*In the Jewish villages of nineteenth-century Russia, drawing
human and animal figures was looked upon as breaking the
Second Commandment and was therefore forbidden.*

He tells it on his deathbed to his eldest son.
It happened when he was still a boy.
Every night after cabbage soup and black bread,
he would sit by the stove in the kitchen
and with a wand of charcoal, God forgive him,
release black horses, rearing and wild,
onto a snowy field. With each stroke
he hears the paper creak and tear.
That doesn't bother him. He always hears
the paper rip along the lines he draws
of mane and flank, belly and hoof,
until the horse stamps on the page in silhouette,
and where the shreds of paper flap
around the outline of the horse's shape
a wind slips through — a wind that smells
of must and clay and decomposing fish.
He recoils from that, for a moment hesitates,
then places his hand on the black-horse shape.
The hand falls through. Damp winds
lick it from a world he doesn't know
and doesn't want to know, and he wakes up
staring at the paper blank upon his lap.
He remembers dimly a whinnying
from a gully somewhere on his right,
where now a broom stands beside the stove,
but that is all. He never finds the horses,
although he can sense them all around
in shadowy corners and darkened rooms,
and every night, as if compelled,
he draws another and sends it

winging off into the midnight air.
God forgive him . . . God forgive . . . He was so young . . .
The last time he saw the horses was the night
the cossacks set fire to the house.
The flames were tossing in the dark
like a mane of blood, and he heard
sinews snapping and cracking bones
as small, charred hooves fell around him in the yard.

THE BARRIER

For hundreds of years the story is the same:
the young man becomes the old man, father to his son.
And because he has traveled once—as peddler,
wagoner, itinerant tailor—he knows:
the Carpathian Mountains are the teeth of the Evil One.
He has seen them close up, whitened with winter,
crammed full like a shark's jaw, barely a foot between peaks.
To pass through to Hungary or Bohemia
is to be swallowed by the Dark One,
who lies with his chin to the earth, mouth open,
waiting for anyone to wander in.
The old man has been close enough to feel that breath,
damp and icy, lay glittering crystals on his coat.

But his sons are restless, no matter what he says.
"Galitsiye and Volhynia are chewing us to rags," they say.
"What is there in Bratzlav or Sadigor that doesn't bite?"
"But here there's family," the old man replies, "people you know,
an uncle in the study house, and God himself looks over all."
"What of Cousin Mendel in Budapest?" a son will say.
"Or Rifka and her husband, who went to Prague," another will put in.
The old man smiles: his face is long,
his teeth are sharp—he's lean as a wolf—
and now he shakes his fingers in a shooing gesture,
raises his chin, and solemnly intones,
"No one's heard a word from them in more than a year."

Outside among cartwheels and dust and flies fat as grapes,
voices bickering and chaff sticking to their sweat,
the sons think their surroundings more dismal than before.
They cannot look at one another, or even look up.
They jam fists into pockets, kick at the street.
Then each raises his head to the west, to the mountains
obscured by miles and mist. A cool breeze sails down.
They shiver. "One day," they think, "one day,"
as each wanders off to his separate house.

THE WOMEN IN THE PHOTOGRAPH

The women are like onions:
layers of wool, linen, and lace
surround an inner self
they are unable to imagine.
Are they only an enclosed dampness,
a skinny sob robed in sour breath?
Mothers, aunts, full-grown sisters:
they sit inside their clothes,
as in this photograph—
corseted, tied, and strapped,
collared to the chin, cuffed
to the wrist, hemmed to the heel—
aware of pressing hoops
and pinching stays
and the tightening grip
of high-buttoned shoes.

Every day they sit and swell,
every day a little wider,
swell around the vague core
none of them can comprehend.
Every day: waiting, waiting
for they can't imagine what,
the taste in their mouths bitter, bitter.
They sigh, groan, shift
in their chairs, even weep.
Aches settle in their backs,
in their elbows, emerge as cramps
in their insteps, tremors in their teeth.

Who are the other women then,
the ones who chop cabbage,
simmer soup, polish furniture
until the furniture glows, unearthly,
like guardian effigies in sacred tombs?

Who are they, then, who bear children,
scold weather, spank sickness
from every cobwebbed corner,
hold on through pillage and rape,
through night after night
of drunken weight upon their breasts?
Can the women in the photograph
be these women too—
women who hold on, hold on,
and will not let go?

GRANDFATHER REMEMBERS HIS YOUTH

Winter

"In winter, the world outside became a universe of glassware,
like the merchandise old Lebenshorn piled on his wagon
that tottered from town to town, jiggling and clinking.
On such nights I'd hold my breath and hope that hush
would keep the trees and lakes and snowy fields,
the iced houses and glazed mud streets from shattering.
God was a glassmaker, just like old Lebenshorn said,
and like men stumbling without candles in the dark
we had to walk on tiptoe through His world
so we wouldn't smash all the goods in His shop."

GRANDFATHER REMEMBERS HIS YOUTH

The Onion

"We had meat once a week, at *Shabbes*,
and then it was bones in the soup.
The rest of the week it was bread,
potatoes, and cabbage in the soup—
and, if we were lucky, an onion.

An onion is a gift from God,
a true Jewish vegetable.
He made it both bitter and sweet,
like the lives of our people,
and so we should never forget
He gave it this power
that allows us to weep unashamed
for all our sorrows and joys."

GRANDFATHER REMEMBERS HIS YOUTH

Leaving Home

"To be dead is to be nothing,
but to be alive is to have all the dead
pushing you from the house
into the sunlight. It is terrible, terrible
to be standing on your porch blinking,
wondering what to do next,
mumbling something or other
like you'll look for a job, get a vodka at the tavern,
sign on some ship as an able-bodied seaman
in the port cities beyond those mountains there.
Whatever you say or choose
seems to make no difference.
And then you realize that you've been wringing
your cap in your hands, and have stood bowed
for all these minutes, all these days and years,
beneath the sun, whose palm
rests warm and comforting on your head."

VILNA, LITHUANIAN RUSSIA, 1892

One of the girls is running through the fields,
the endless fields of stubble and mud
that spread like an ashen goose-feather quilt
from horizon to horizon beneath a lowering sky.
She runs, and you can't see her face,
but you know she's unmarried and young.
It's the free, almost frenzied way
her knees kick at her skirts, there
under a raw gray day so close to winter
she must be running toward another season.
Do you hear, as she hears, the wind pulled back
like hair over her ears? Her heart is an egg
where the unborn bounce and lurch, impatient
to be born, as wild as she is.

                          Her blood?

Her blood, her blood—the pulse unspools
and she runs free;
                          but by nightfall it rewinds again
and draws her back to the house in town
where two sisters and five brothers glower,
where the old man sits at the table saying grace,
and her mother mutters that she hasn't cleaned the house,
that none of them help—the children,
her husband's mother, the milkless cow:
it's a daily headache, it can't go on,
and so help her, as God is good, things will change.
Her swollen ankles, her varicose veins,
her eyes contracted to needle points—
it's all too much. As she's her mother's child,
she'll change their ways, or kill the lot.

Later, in bed between sisters who grumble and snore,
the girl slides a fingertip along the thin blue vein
paying out from her wrist and up her arm

and imagines her run. Now she flies
over fields and moon-lidded lakes—forests here, towns there,
a river's silver stream unwinding through the dark.
Her blood turns cold, then silver, and rolls through the fields
to where the rustling ocean waits, but the ocean
is somewhere in the dark where she can't see,
somewhere beyond the horizon of her dreams.

The endless plains around her like the years—
whose daughter is this? Whose mother will she be?
Where has she gone, this girl?
What landscape is she dreaming now?

GRANDMOTHER-GRANDFATHER

Out of the dust and flies,
out of the bustle on the street,
she suddenly appears.
He has been loading iron
on a wagon for his uncle.
Her hooped skirt, her long black hair—
she seems to glide, buoyant,
along the sidewalk, turning a deaf ear
to all the slamming and shouting
in the road. But he, the young man
who has never thought of women—
except the unbuttoned, sweaty breasts
of meaty tavern whores—
who has never thought of home and child,
stands astonished in her wake.
The flies, the voices, the street
for an instant seem to evaporate,
and before that tumult can rush back in,
he knows he's seen the woman
who will be his wife.

She does not see him then,
but strolls back home and helps
her mother plan the evening meal.
They have servants. Her father
deals in oil and grain;
his brother owns a mill.
She has gone to the *gymnasium*
and can read and write,
her father's little *barishnya*.
Two days later, a friend
informs her that someone,
a disheveled young man
in dusty workman's clothes,
has been following them everywhere.
At the next corner,

a fluttering in her chest,
she turns her head to see.
And what she sees—the lean face,
the lanky body and arms,
the knobby outsized hands—
"just grabbed mine breath avay."

Why do everyone's grandparents
fall in love like this?
And why can't their children
or their children's children
as easily find a mate?
"Times vere simpler then,"
the old man says, while she,
nodding, always preoccupied,
snaps pea pods in a mixing bowl.
"Come on, what really happened?
Nobody falls in love like that!"
They pause, turn to one another,
and smiling, say no more,
as if they formed a wall together
called Grandmother-Grandfather.

Behind this wall are broken things—
rusty axles, barrels, carts—
where bearded men stagger through the snow,
whipped by anonymous horsemen
through blizzards that extend
as far as the mind can imagine,
coming to rest where the wind slows
and a honeyed light
falls through a cabin window
onto an open book. Bodies
hurry in the shadows, cursing
and sighing, as they pack for a journey
that the older ones recall
is similar to another trek
their grandparents made years before.

The Marriage Agreement

Vilna, 1898

She is a granddaughter of an obscure disciple
of the Gaon, Elijah ben Rabbi Solomon,
praise his holy, most glittering name.
Or so the father claims. That is nothing new.
The poorest laborer will boast that some scholar
or some illustrious Hassid has sprung from his ancestral blood,
although he isn't sure of the ancestor's town or name.

The young man sits and listens with an upright back,
his lean face, high cheekbones, and smoke-dense eyes
so impassive, so unblinking, his features seem engraved.
When the bald little man is still, the young man
precedes his reply by turning his head slowly to the side,
until, in profile, it lies against the window light,
a wolf's head in silhouette. The little man sucks in his breath.

"As for me," the young man says, as if he hasn't heard,
"I have no ancestors worthy to tickle the hairs in your ears.
I'm an Ashkenazi, of course, like you,
but what's that? Dollars and cents is what you want
and what I haven't got. But look, Mister,
Mister Misnagid Wheat Dealer Man, my family's come through.
Some say that my grandfather fed at the teats of a wolf
when he fell from a sleigh one winter night
and was lost in the steppes for a week;
and that my uncles are tavern men who break heads all day;
and that we're not so distantly related
to Misha Yaponchik, who in Odessa is called the king
because—for a fee—he protects the Moldavanka Jews
against every cossack, cop, and government flunky.
If that's so, then a marriage alliance with me
would be worth it to you. I'll be honest:

I'm no stranger to violence, but I'm a hardworking man who just wants his share. And I'm plain-talking, too: your daughter could do worse. And so could you."

A Theory of Genetics

Take a small plump woman with skin
as white and soft as a bun –
a gentle woman, not timid really,
but mild as an early April sun,
wed her to a lean man, a lanky man
with long jaw and outsized hands,
and these are the sons:

                    short and thick
with hands and feet as small as girls' –
not brawlers really but boys
with round heads balanced on squat necks,
who'll never turn their boots from a fight.
Only the eldest has his father's hands and height.
As for the girls, one daughter is massive, not fat,
solid as the furniture she sits on,
waiting for the husband who will take her
to a household of her own. The other daughter
is as slim and long-legged as a boy.

Ah, God's ways are truly strange: He reached
into each of these children's unformed genes,
like an old man rummaging inside a tin
for a pinch of snuff, and this was the result.
Even God, it seems, can make mistakes,
and heaven knows He made them with these Jews,
who look part cossack and part Pole,
part Ukrainian hooligan or Russian lout –
the outsized hands, the tiny feet,
the shortened bodies and the lanky ones.
Even the bun-like woman and her tall lean man
are not quite right,

                  and the error, really,
is not to be found in some divine quirk

twitching cryptically in their genes,
but in burning villages and roaring men:
cossacks, Ukrainians, Russians off the farm,
clubbing, stabbing, running people through,
ransacking houses, shattering shops,
and pressing down into the squirming skin
beneath linen and lace. Their trousers
around their ankles, they thrust on their knees,
as century after century they grunt out their seed.

Grandmother's Secret

Once she tells her youngest daughter,
"If in Russia we had divorce,
I wouldn't be with him now—never.
Like a tree, your papa—he doesn't bend."

So she became a breeze, her long hair loose,
bowing and scooting just out of reach
when he shook his branches at her
or roared like a storm.

                              "He never once
raised his hands—never—and would bring
from the market fans and lace. And plums,
plums he'd steal with his own hands
from peasant trees and hide in his shirt,
'for his eternal bride,' he'd say and grin."
When she told her daughter this, she cried.

"But after the first month, I never loved him.
I was running always to and from his voice
while he sits and sits in his chair
and says 'Bring, bring—get, get.'
When I think of that house,
I am always running from shelf to shelf,
wall to wall, like from inside
I could never get out, never breathe in the sun."

"What did you want from marriage, Mama?"

The old woman tilts her head and thinks,
then shrugs. "Not this. Plums! Plums!
But does he ever share with me his heart!
He is a stranger asleep in the bed,
something for me to lean against, like a door."

"Then why do you stay?" her daughter asks.

The old woman sighs, and turns away.
"Without him, what would become of me?" she says;
and, more softly, so the girl can hardly hear,
"And without me, what would become of him?"

DEPARTURE

I
How does it happen? How does it come about?
The heat, the flies, the dust, the icy roads
that year after year are folded away
like clothes in an attic trunk:
this is the way it has been for her parents and his
and their parents' parents before they were born.
How does it happen then? How does it come about?

Does she read it somewhere? Does he
hear about it in the square?

                              There is talk
of war in that world out there, there always is:
talk that the cossacks will ride once more
or the Black Hundreds come. But the peasants
remain civil, unless they are drunk,
and the years flit by like pages in a book.

So how does it happen? How do they learn
that beyond their house on the edge of a wooden town
surrounded by dust and wind and an endless plain,
somewhere on the other side of the dark,
the glittering gold cities of America lie?

And what is the talk between them – the weeks,
the months, the years of endless talk
in all those huddled huts and houses,
where every village building seems to whisper?
What is the talk that eventually blows them,
like clothes on the wind, to foreign harbors,
where they sit on bundles at the end of the pier:
the women, as bulky as the bales around them,
in shawls and kerchiefs, smelling like damp onions;
the men, in round black hats with wide brims,

smoking clay pipes—all of them silent, still,
all of them looking out to sea?

How does it happen? How does it come about?

2

Where have they come from? The townspeople aren't sure.
Every dawn the strangers are there at the end of the pier,
and they are still there at noon, and then at dusk,
sitting on crates and baling wire, belongings
piled around them, while boys and girls,
all dressed like their elders, dash among them,
as if, like the bales and crates, the elders
were part of the pier.
                            And they remain there,
untying bundles in the violet evening,
breaking open bread and biting into onions
with elaborate slowness and care.

Later that night, when the townspeople
look from their bedroom windows,
they find that a great ship has arrived.
Strings of light bulbs, swinging in the breeze,
climb into the dark in glittering pyramids,
and the bluish-white spheres of innumerable portholes
dip below floodlights that pierce the night
with crisscrossing shafts of misty light,
so that one senses more than sees an ocean liner,
swaying, immobile, somewhere in their midst.

Next morning the liner is gone, and the strangers with it.
And every morning, in rain or sun, it is the same:
new strangers gather where the old ones sat.
Hamburg, Rotterdam, Antwerp, Bremen:
does the port's location make a difference?
The strangers depart as surely as they arrive—
from harbors that do not need a name,
on ships most people do not remember,
for a destination no one can be sure of.

The Crossing (1909)

1

He sneaks across the border near Grodno,
lugging a black leather satchel
crammed with family heirlooms
entrusted by relatives to his care.
In-laws, uncles, aunts—
their sighs and whisperings
are a presence dragging at his hand
and pushing at his back,
even on board *Der Staatendam*,
the freighter bucking through the waves
from Bremen to New York.

2

With two hundred men, he's pitched
about the cargo hold, vomits and sleeps
on a mattress made of straw,
listens to the others moan,
and then moans too. He cannot pull
his body from the wooden bunk
to go on deck. He stinks
of sweat and fear, smelling sourness
like blotches of mildew in his body hair.
He clutches the satchel, feels often
for the knife in his boot,
and even in delirium refuses to relax.
Lice cover him like petty worries
he always thought he was above,
and like the others he soon forgets
"the golden buildings of New York."
Now his universe is steel plates
that shudder overhead; his stars,
rivet heads that stitch the sky
into sections as meaningless
as they are exact.

3

            For days
the men lie in their bunks, staring up.
Several older ones succumb
to what the ship's physician calls
failure of the heart. *Failure*
of purpose, the lean man thinks
and that night feeds his body
with rage at his weakness
and everyone's, finally dragging
the satchel stair by stair on deck.
Alone in the dark, he stands
on the staggering ship,
jabbing his wolf's jaw
at the icy swipes of spray,
until— clothes drenched,
bones veering and shifting
like a stack of plates—
he howls with anguish and glee.

4

Below, he turns his mattress over,
rebinds the straw, washes,
and shines his shoes, as others
lift their heads and watch.
One gets up and combs his beard,
and then another, until all of them
are mimicking his routine
and following his movements with their eyes.
He wants none of that, but what can he do?
He growls at them and glares.
But when they ask him to moderate
a meeting to list complaints
about their treatment aboard ship,
he consents, sitting in their midst
as they bicker, argue, stop, look to him
and wait, finally forgetting he's there
when he remains silent and withdrawn,

unable to comprehend the words
clamoring around his head
like seabirds around a wave-fringed rock.

5

At Ellis Island, he is ignored.
After all, he is a peasant,
not a rabbi, businessman, or scholar.
Besides, they're pushed and pulled,
chalked and examined by endless hands
before they're allowed to go.
For some, relatives are waiting,
and they run to them. But others,
perhaps remembering, nod as they pass.
There is no one to meet him,
and he refuses to turn his head
as he strides with the satchel
toward the ferry slip, surprised
by the skyline across the river.
Those are not the bulbous spires
of Russian churches, or the smoke-stained
timbers of stunted tenements,
but throngs of skyscrapers made of stone,
rising flat and slim, all edges
in the smoky, early-morning sun.
He senses more than knows
that a continent unrolls
somewhere beyond the city:
lakes, woods, mountains, plains
rise and fall away, curving
with the contour of the planet;
and in all that land
there is no one he knows.

PART 2

THE NEW WORLD

THE IMMIGRANT

He'll work for no one.
"Such a man," the uncles
grumble. "Such a man."
"Six years!" he says,
unbuttoning a cuff
and rolling up his sleeve.
Six years bending over a machine,
pressing knee pants and jackets,
until his eyes go bad
and he can't raise his head
without lifting up this arm.
"Six years!" he'll say
and show the arm
as if it told the story.
Son of horse dealers
in the Ukraine,
horse breaker himself,
he is a *luftmensch*, according
to his in-laws, a man of air,
one who has no substance,
no steady occupation
to argue for his *yikhus*,
his status or worth.
"He'll ride the wind,
if the wind is of his liking,
and pick up jobs
that keep him out-of-doors
and other men's employ,"
or so the uncles grumble.

But for six years
he bit his mustache,
living in one closet room
while working in another,

saving for a house in Brooklyn
and passage for his wife and kids.

After that, he'll work for no one.
He keeps a cow and chickens
in the yard, and a female goat.
"My *farm*," he tells his sons
when they say "house;"
and sells eggs and pails of milk
around the neighborhood.
It is 1916-17.
While Europe boils with war
and revolution, men with pushcarts
ply the neighborhoods of Brooklyn
with fruit and vegetables,
cloth, ribbons, pots and pans,
singing their wares
in answering voices
that cross and recross
for several blocks.

One day he shows up
with a horse and cart,
and paints a sign
that offers any child
a chance to prance
through Canarsie
for just a penny.
It doesn't make much money,
but now he has a horse
to haul the milk and eggs.
Now he has a horse.

From that day on, at sunset,
he unhitches the horse,
and mounts, and canters
high and lordly
through Canarsie's

still uncluttered streets,
so much the long-limbed cossack
that as he passes,
bearded men cower and mumble.
Dismounting at Jamaica Bay,
he looks at that darkening,
violet expanse, remembers
the pale sunlight
on the cobbled streets
of Minsk, the six years
pressing pants and coats,
or the number of eggs
he's sold that day,
before he slips
onto the horse once more
and, turning a straight back
to the sea, trots home.

MOTHER REMEMBERS HER EIGHTH WINTER

All winter long,
she and her brothers
steal to the train yard
just after dark
to pick coal from the tracks,
careful not to clatter it
in the scuttle
lest the watchman come.
So cold, she thinks
the nights have frozen
and cracked, and each
blue-black chunk
is a piece of fallen sky.

At home she sees the burning
in the kitchen stove—
orange flowers
blossoming from the black,
and knows that heaven
warms her. Then,
before bed, she runs
to the window and watches
the thick gray smoke
she and her brothers
have provided ascend
from the rooftop
to fill the cracks
beneath the glittering
black floor
of God's palace.

Father and Son

His body is long,
his face is long and thin.
Overhung eyebrows and smoke-black eyes,
and darkened hollows under cheekbones and chin.
His teeth are white fangs,
and even when he is seventy-one, they look like this.
When he smiles,
they slide into view,
and make the boy cringe:
the old man has a wolf in him.

The old man's eldest son
looks much the same:
beard too heavy; mouth too grim.
There is something definitely foreign in each of them.
Angered, they'll growl and snap,
pinch the offender's arms or ears
and fling him toward another room
with a boot in the buttocks or a final slap.

That's for family, inside the house.
For the bickerers and bargainers on the street,
there are the smoke-dense eyes and the toothy grin.
And should those outsiders cheat or curse,
there's the knife in the boot —
or knobby knuckles hurtling toward their chins.
To others the world is dog-eat-dog,
but the old man and his eldest are wolves,
and they'll hear none of that.

Besides, they're taking care:
the family and all its heirlooms
are in their charge: brooches and tarnished spoons,
a pearl necklace from a great-aunt's will,
several silver plates and cups.

They are neither kind nor heroic men:
they mean to survive.
That's what the old man's parents taught to him,
and he teaches it to his daughters and sons
with such ferocity they cannot look him in the eye.
Love is not the point—it never was.
Joy and ecstasy are bearded men in black,
who caper through the streets like laundry flapping on a line.
Power, control—that's what he's after.
Saliva sluices through his teeth, his eyes flash.
When he dreams of God, he tells his eldest son,
he envisions a hand that holds the world like a rock
about to be thrown at a noise in the dark.
The portion of rock covered by this hand
is shadowy: night. The portion that isn't,
all that bird song and light—"Vel,"
the old man says, "who cares about dhat."

FOOD

The remedy for everything is food.
For backache, have a plum.
For menstrual cramps, a pear.
For heartache or any fevers in the blood,
soup—thick, yellow, chicken soup
with glinting globules of fat.
For those gone tipsy in the head,
not herbs and roots that aunts and widows,
guided by the moon, once ripped from fields
beyond the outskirts of the town,
but "a balanced diet"—
steak, potatoes, salad,
and "a piece of fruit."
Now any decision is best resolved
following a night's sleep
that inevitably follows "a good meal."
If you feel bad, have something to eat.
If you feel good, celebrate by eating more.

In summer, winter, his mother,
at the boy's elbow, serving from a pan,
urges him to eat, eat more,
reciting an endless menu
of chicken, liver, beef
"for making power in the body;"
halibut, flounder, sole
"for making power in the brain;"
and spinach, peaches, prunes
"for making sure the bowels
run regular, like trains."

"The memories of hunger grew,"
his grandfather says,
"until the body vas an empty place
demanding to be filled,

39

as if from one age to the other
the cells have been housing
the hungers of the dead,
and now, in this place of plenty,
the dead are crying out,
demanding their due."

DINNER AT GRANDPA'S

The tablecloth spreads like a bed sheet between them.
It is as white as the black-whiskered knuckles
the old man holds in front of his face.
But it is the teeth, slashing, luminous,
ripping at the meat, that the small boy sees.
"So eat, eat," the old man says,
stirring the air with glistening fingers,
the teeth still chewing as he speaks.
They gleam like chips of ice behind his lips.
"Can this be our Rochele's son?" the teeth intone,
a hand pointing with a bone as if it were a wand.
"Leave the boy alone," the plump old woman says.
Has she been there all along? The old man grunts,
shakes out at her the slippery fingernails
of his other hand as if it were a handkerchief.
She disappears.

                        The boy lifts a meat-thick bone
and bites, seeing the other mouth pause
as his teeth rip flesh, shred fibers,
sink through grease and fat.
He is aware at each bite of his jaw's impact,
the hinged weight swinging up like a battering ram.
Below the mask he doesn't remember putting on,
he can sense a blunt bone face he doesn't recognize.
Each jolt, each dental thud is resonant
and echoes everywhere through his head,
as if his cranium is the dome that surrounds the universe.
But the dome is cracked: shreds of black membrane
hang and flap like wallpaper from its sides.
A red wing tip stabs through a chink,
clouds of static rumble beyond the rim,
and only by working his teeth until his jaws ache
can the boy keep those clouds backed up

and the universe safe within.
When he looks up, he finds the old man's mouth has shut,
and with slumping shoulders and a wistful grin,
the old man is smiling across the yards of tablecloth at him.

The Poet at Three

His Talents Recognized

It is a stranger's house,
a long living room in shadows,
spurs of sunlight
on glass and porcelain,
and beyond the two glass doors
paths and statues
in a sun-struck forest.
With his back to the doors,
the boy is seated
on what he thinks
is a table, a table
like a tarnished mirror—
so polished yet so dim
he can hardly see his face in it.
The table drops away
on all sides, like an island
that everywhere ends in cliffs.
It is a table
with no chairs around it,
should he slip. He is so high,
so far away from Mommy,
he doesn't want to fall,
and huddling in the island's center
plays with the new brown shoes
that hide his toes.
His mother and uncles
are chatting somewhere
in the shadows, and when they stop
and he looks up,
he is staring at the old man
with the starched white face
who had been introduced
as the owner of the house,
a "distant relative"

and "famous concert pianist."
The man must be standing on his knees
before the table:
only his head and shoulders
can be seen, like a moon
risen over one side
of the island. A trembling begins,
and the boy feels skittering edges
hurtle up his feet and legs.
It is as though there is
a seething run of water
all around, and that is followed
by the rumble and the boom
of waves driven by typhoons
and hurricanes. The island quakes;
it bounces from within.
He will be pitched into the sea
that now so angrily engulfs him.
Then there is a scream above the waves.
A gull, he thinks at first,
a gull in the wind, then realizes
that the scream is his.
"Fortissimo!" the white-faced moon
calls out. "What exquisite counterpoint.
Chopin would have marveled!"
And as suddenly as it began,
the sea withdraws, and so does the man.
An uncle emerges from the gloom,
shaking a finger like a bone rattle.
"What an honor! Did you hear?
Now don't you ever forget!"
But the boy is lost somewhere
inside his skin, as when his mother
tugs a sweater over his head
but can't get it off and he is hugged
by a darkness so close
it wrestles the breath from his chest
and squeezes the screams from his throat.

CONVALESCENCE

The apartment house is thirty stories high
and faces Central Park. But here, on a side street
always half in shadow, the boy peers
from his bedroom window on the second floor
at a factory in the loft across the way.
Below, there is a warehouse loading dock
where trucks rumble and snort in a metal din:
sealed barrels, crates, and cartons
are hauled down or lifted up and shouldered in.
The men in undershirts are all forearms and grins
and wave at him, while the women they whistle at
prance around packing cases and do not look back.
Every day he hoists his face to the windowsill
to watch these men, and to observe the old ladies
who totter behind terriers, or those women, like his mother,
who clack down the street and seem not to hear
the whistles trailing after them.

Crossing the street in a buttoned gray suit,
his father glances at these men and quickly turns away,
then looks up at the boy, but neither waves nor grins.
Entering the apartment, he yells in the kitchen,
never saying a word to the boy in the bedroom beyond—
that lettuce, that cabbage head
left out to rot on the windowsill
by his wife once again. How many times has he told her
to put it in the icebox, or at least out of sight?
They aren't living in the slums any more.
"And another thing: when are you going to tell
that *meshuggener* old man to stop filling the kid's head
with tales of Russia. He's been in America
for over thirty years, and —"
Two of the men in undershirts drag a barrel from a truck,
shadows curling where their muscles tense and shift.
Both stop to stare after a passing woman,

then turn, shake their heads, and grin.
The redheaded one looks up, points at the woman's back,
and waves. The boy, impassive as always,
feels his small hand flutter as it rises above his head.

THE MIRROR

The boy looks in the mirror often, not to view his face
but to look into the room that is now behind him:
coffee table, plum-colored easy chairs, and couch,
where the old man plucks threads
from the golden throw pillow on his lap
and the boy's mother and father sit.
It is as though he stares into another room,
a room where he has never been, and is not known,
and can observe his mother glancing from her magazine
to his father seated like a stranger in a railroad car
and the old man pulling at the pillow threads
like a furious harpist who cannot sit still.
And they remain that way until the boy turns around
and is with them again, like a doctor
entering the waiting room from an inner office door.

THE GIFT

Gladiolas like orange flames
in the florist's window.
The boy buys two with three nickels
and carries them like a torch
toward home. They light his way
through an afternoon
gray and overcast,
where people smile
and turn as he goes
as if they'd follow him
to a similar afternoon—
their own mother's birthday.
Her birthday, yes,
but is she older? Never!
Each year she remains the same.
The gladiolas are to thank her
for staying as she is,
for being "mommy's age."
He marches up the stairs,
clomping his shoes, holding
the tall stems upright
in their crinkly green wrapping.
"Oh," she says, "oh," clasps hands
in front of her chest,
eyes watering, and rushes
for the cut-glass vase.

From a dream that night,
he hears his father say,
"Secret admirer, huh?"
and laugh, but the laughter
is tight in his throat,
as if he were gagging,
and the boy smiles in his sleep.

The Poet at Five

Waiting

At the age of five, he realizes everyone is waiting.
Rocking back and forth on the couch, muttering prayers,
his grandfather snaps his head erect
and, with an eyebrow cocked above an eye
that gleams like a lump of coal,
peers into a doorway or a corner.
At times, the old man's prayer shawl
flutters on his shoulders as if about to take wing
and fly him to another world.
The boy's father, with loosened tie and open collar,
rubs his hands on both sides of a towel,
as if he had Aladdin's lamp inside,
and looks out the window at the evening city sky.
And Mother is always staring through walls,
trying to see into paintings or neighbors' closets,
and when she glances at the boy, her eyes softening,
she seems to look at something in his head
he hadn't known was there.

                                         Even the janitor,
when he lifts his cap and wipes his forehead
after rolling a can of cinders from the cellar,
stares down the street as if an accident
is about to happen, or his brother from Poland,
whom he hasn't heard from in years,
is about to turn the corner.

                                     And the butchers,
the bored cashiers, the harried candy-store owners
every now and then look up
when someone passes on the street
and continue to stare at nothing specific,
after whomever it was has gone.
When the boy looks where they do,

49

he sees nothing and soon despairs,
for none of them talk about what they are waiting for,
except his grandfather, who whispers of the Evil One,
of three spits *here* and of sacred words muttered *there*.

It is not until his father leaves for work one day
and does not come back, and he begins to gaze
at walls and pavement squares, and one day sees,
on his paint-chipped bedroom ceiling, murals of marchers,
decrepit and old, with hands uplifted to the sky,
that the boy can accept the glances and stares.
He still can't explain why everyone is waiting,
but he is comforted by two images
that swarm and blend with the shadows
sliding across the bedroom ceiling.
In one, the marchers shake their fists and curse.
In the other, the one he prefers,
plump rabbis and skinny scholars sing rapturously
of what's past and passing and to come,
and dare to jig on spikes of fire.

The New Apartment House

There is a war somewhere, and his father is gone,
but here, now, there are the halls and stairs
of the new apartment house. The lobby floor
is a maroon-and-white mosaic garden, its tiles
reminiscent of his mother's Persian rug.
But the tiles are cracked and scarred,
the floor pocked with gaps. Maroon runners,
resembling forest paths, lead the boy
past urns and potted plants to an elevator
big and bronze as a bank door, but as slow
as a bent grandma lowering herself into a chair.
He watches the gilt dial limp endlessly
from right to left, as if marking the sun's progress
across the sky, and when the door rolls back
out waddles that wart-faced witch
Mrs. Solomon, muttering curses about the Evil Eye;
or, like the black hull of a pirate ship,
a baby carriage pushes its prow into the hall.
The boy prefers to climb the stairs to the apartment
where he lives with his mother and uncle,
although he spends his days near the lobby plants
flying the airplane at the end of his arm,
marching his soldiers from cigar-box forts,
or watching the German janitor limp and mutter
as he mops the hall or drags ash cans full of cinders
from the darkness beyond the basement door.
At times, the boy examines marbles from his pouch
just like a jeweler; or he lifts one to the light
as though he could see the inner workings of a world in it,
if he looked close enough and held his breath.

Sometimes he prowls the halls and stairwells,
lighted only by grime-gray windows on each floor,
and plays find-the-treasure or surprise-the-gnome.
Or he trails the older boys, all nine and ten,

who rush past to the cellar in a loose-knit gang,
or push him in the chest and tell him, "Blow!"
One day in early summer, the janitor's blond-haired son,
with the other boys peering from behind his back,
grabs the boy's arm and says, "Jew, come here!"
The boy shakes free and runs upstairs,
where his mother, cradling his face in her palms,
tells him that "a man can't hide behind a woman,"
and holds him close before she pushes him out the door.
Wrestled to the floor, he is carried, kicking,
to the basement, where cinders crunch underfoot
and the fiery furnace god, now cool and somber,
shudders only an occasional breath
of gases and ashes, vinegar and bits of bone.
Here the boy is thrown to the floor,
unbuttoned and exposed to all those eyes
looking down at him. The janitor's son
points and kicks the breath from his chest.
"Jew!" he shouts again and again,
as he straddles the boy's ribs
and beats him in the face with his fists.
All the while, the boy's mother stands
weeping behind the apartment door.
But the boy won't learn of that for years.
When he rises and staggers from the cellar,
all he will know is the laughter behind him
as he wanders through the once-familiar halls.

Uncle Abe

I

By silent agreement, no one in the family
is allowed to speak his name—
this uncle, short and nondescript,
with round face and rubbery nose,
who lived with them in 1941.
His handmade suits—dark brown
and banker's gray—though elegant
did not attract the young boy's gaze
as did the metal eyeglass frames
flashing from behind his ears
and circling his pale blue eyes
in channeled streams of gold.

Each day he shaved with the boy.
Without his gold-rimmed glasses,
he squinted at the bathroom mirror
as if trying to discern the shape
that lumbered toward him
through the steam. The boy's razor
was empty, a gift from this uncle
against the day when he became a man.
But the uncle's razor cut both ways,
and he left one day with a jaunty wave,
never to return, hauling his hand
and everyone's memory of him
out the door.

              Six years later,
when the boy is twelve, he dreams this uncle
stealing through the bedroom window,
less a prowler than a Santa Claus.
"There was this man," he tells his aunt.
"He wore glasses made of gold
which flashed in the dark . . ."

But he gets no further than that,
for his aunt staggers against the icebox
and clutches her heart. Even the big uncles,
who never look down but stride past shops
with everyone staring at their backs,
twitch when he mentions the name,
as if they were punched in the chest,
and weep as they walk down the street
without wiping the tears away.

2

"Yes," says Cousin Leo at the handball court,
"but never mention him to your mom,"
and he brings the shaving memories back
when he tells the boy the story.
By silent agreement, no one in the family
is allowed to speak this uncle's name:
He was Abe, just Abe, the name shortened
in America, no longer biblical,
no longer recalling the patriarch
who must sacrifice his son
until an angel sent by God
at the last moment intercedes
and proclaims a covenant
by which Abraham's descendants
shall be as numerous as the stars
and the nations of the earth
shall consider themselves blessed
to have his heirs as citizens.

Abe's angel, it turns out, was Irish
or Italian, and interceded
with two bullets in the back of the head
to separate him from his life
and from the one hundred thousand
he was carrying from a poker game.
Abe, "the policy king of Brooklyn,"
ran a numbers racket on his own,

employing more than two hundred men,
and controlled two restaurants on the side.

For eight years he ruled the family,
while the old man, ill, huddled near the stove.
Streetwise and intelligent, this uncle
banked millions under aliases
he entrusted to no one, refused to marry
because sharing a life such as his,
he told his mother, was unfair to any woman,
and gave away at least as much money
to brothers, beggars, charities, and friends
as he did to judges and cops.

Eventually the police unearth the satchel,
but not the money or the triggerman.
The newspapers call this uncle an example
of "the immigrant's dilemma,"
and label him "a modern Robin Hood."

All this means nothing to the family,
who cannot understand why one so kind
should be cut off so young.
To them he remains uncle, son, and brother,
whose name they remember but refuse to say.

3
Who were you, Uncle? The newspapers
say one thing, the family another.
Did family tradition lead you to the rackets,
some fly speck in your chromosomes
that swarms through me? In another time
would you have followed the life of the mind
toward which your gentle eyes inclined?
Or did you pursue the same pragmatic hopes,
stripped of morality, which drove the old man
from the snows of southern Russia
to the tenements of New York?

Questions addressed to the wind
come back on the wind unanswered,
and the only words anyone remembers
you saying—"If you want something
from someone, kiss his ass.
When he wants something from you,
he'll kiss yours"—tell nothing,
provide only a momentary glimpse of you,
and, ironically, like your life and fortune
and the circumstances of your unsolved death,
by balancing both phrases, rub themselves out.

In time the family accepted your death
as a corrupted New World version
of your biblical namesake's life,
where the angel sent by God arrived too late,
and where you were son and father both—
father to your short-lived youth.
There was also the fear,
an almost palpable foreboding,
that whoever did the killing
would come back to annihilate
brother, nephew, aunt—the entire family,
one by one—like an avenging angel
whose mission no one could comprehend.
As a result, the family agreed
that no one would speak your name
or seek the ones responsible for your death,
hoping that would end it, and it did.

Now you are a picture in a scrapbook—
those brooding eyes, that relentless stare.
And when a nephew or a grandchild
comes upon your fading photograph,
you are identified as someone who died young
and left no son to intercede for him.

MOTHER

I

She is a luminous kite
sailing in the sky,
connected to him
by the telephone wire,
a light in the heavens
for him to steer by
no matter how the winds
tumble and toss.
She is up there each night
with dance bands, wine glasses,
and applause on the radio.
And "Mommy? Mommy?" he calls
from the darkened boarding schools.
He could see her from the window,
if the matron would let him look.
But after every call,
it's always "Get to bed!"
the French teacher
twisting an ear
or the math instructor
rapping knuckles on his skull.

The voice on the telephone
has a life of its own.
It rumbas in Miami,
dines in Frisco or L.A.,
smells of wild gardenia
and Chanel, chimes
with gold and rubies,
and is wrapped in furs.
That voice is geography,
a distance to be mapped
from the center of his chest
to Hot Springs, Chicago,

Montreal – a distance
over lakes and townships
where the moon rides
between his voice and hers.

2

Where to find her.
In pocketbooks on closet shelves,
among bobby pins and pennies?
In those deflated dresses
still exhaling perspiration
mixed with wild gardenia?
Or beyond the chiming hangers,
past the door he imagines
in the rear of the closet
that opens on another country,
where furtive shopboys
and men with sweaty faces
come to hack at the land
for gold or wheat
but kneel before her.
She accepts their tributes
with a nod, making sure,
when he is there, that the boy
observes her condescension,
as if it revealed a secret knowledge
only he is allowed to share.
But she forgets he is a man
and like the others covets her
and cannot understand
what her expression means;
and so they quarrel on the telephone
until the distance between them
is greater than he can comprehend.

3
Grandma-Baba said that she was always beautiful.
Even in Vilna when she was six,
even then men would follow her with their eyes.
Later she strode through the markets of Brooklyn,
shaking her long black hair and laughing.
The old woman waddled to keep up, laughing too,
although she didn't know at what,
while shop boys gawked, and butchers and grocery men,
chewing on matches behind their windows,
stared at the girl with their eyes half-shut.

Tall and slim, she quits school at twelve,
ashamed at always standing last in line.
At fifteen, posing in a bathing costume,
she wins the Coney Island Beauty Contest,
and her father beats her for that.
At seventeen, she is in Manhattan,
modeling in the garment trade,
two years away from marriage and a son.
Brooklyn is behind her, beyond the river,
beyond the Bridge and the tall buildings
in Borough Hall and Nevins Street
and the house on Avenue B where her parents
live like ghosts behind their window shades.

Not that she stays away. She visits
almost every afternoon, listening to complaints,
counting out hundred-dollar bills
so a niece can have an operation,
or sending the chauffeur with the cream-colored Cord
to drive her nephew and his friends,
with bats and gloves, to the neighborhood schoolyard.
At other times, she brings food and clothes,
and twice each month, while her mother nods
and her father huddles near the stove,
she removes her mink, and on hands and knees,
scrubs the hallway and the kitchen floor.

4
Who were you really, Mother?
The ghetto immigrant who shuffled
English and Yiddish on her tongue?
The beauty queen whose ripening body
brushed against the lusts of men
but who never felt her own blood lurch
in response to any of them?
The girl who never allowed love
to sting her sight but was blinded
by mirrors all her life?
The old woman who creeps
from room to room, muttering worries
about her middle-aged son?

Princess, wicked queen, witch,
you were all of those and none—
images a small boy conjured
from his picture books.
When I searched the closet,
pushed past gowns and furs,
all I found was a wall—hard, cold,
without a hidden door,
another country, or you;
and so I cut the wire
on the telephone, and you fell
to earth like empty clothes.

5
                    Mother,
although you shift and change
like clothes on a wash line
that the wind tries on
again and again,
I continue to think of you
as I did when young,
on those nights when I called to you
over and over in the dark.

Somehow you were always near,
a presence even when gone,
so I knew I wasn't an orphan
and was compelled to search for you,
wondering what I'd done wrong.
That's why I was a bad boy,
bad and then delinquent.
Waiting in those darkened schools
huddled beneath the sky—
beneath those miles of wind and moon—
I never thought I'd see
your eyes again, or breathe
the perfume in your hair.
That's why I didn't eat
but smashed the carrots on my plate,
and why I was still at the table,
forced to chew the mash I'd made,
long after the other kids
had been sent to bed. I never knew
if you were coming back. Never.
That's why I didn't learn to read
until I was ten, or to memorize
my times tables until two years later,
and why my anger multiplied
You times You times You times You
which equaled nothing, nothing
but the voice I waited for each night
to ring out its arrival and to speak
from all those moon-spun miles away:
voice that tempted me
to scream and throw my food,
or to knock the other children down,
even to bite the teachers' legs,
when it *shushed* me and said
you loved me always but didn't know
when you could visit me again.

6

What did I want from you,
and what could you give?
Bodily warmth? Serenity?
The knowledge that you moved
among tables and chairs,
arranging plates and spoons
in the very next room?
I cannot put into words
what I expected as a boy,
and whatever you could give
I no longer need. And yet,
in person or on the phone,
I still appear before you
like a suppliant, hoping
for an act, a gesture, a sign,
something, anything from you,
here in the enclosing night
where I'm surrounded by the scent
of dried gardenias—
still hushed, still waiting,
still holding my breath.

7

Once more we talk long-distance,
both looking for words
to shrink the continent. Our words
create landmarks in the night,
signposts naming junctures and turnings,
remembered places on a map
not yet complete and constantly changing,
while the moon flies over freeways, farms,
cities resembling overturned jewel boxes,
and headlights prowling the roads
as if hunting for something lost
or not yet discovered.

THE SEARCH

Blessed art Thou, O Lord, our God,
King of the Universe
Who bringeth forth bread from the earth.

—THE JEWISH PRAYER FOR BREAD

Spending a weekend with relatives
near a truck farm in New Jersey,
he asks if that is where God plants the bread.
His cousins laugh, and later he steals away
to watch the loaves emerge from the furrows.
"What you want here, kid? Go home . . . Go on!"

A year later, when he is six,
Mommy sends him to the bake shop,
and *there* is the King of the Universe
in apron and undershirt.
He is five-foot-one and fat,
with sweaty strands of slick black hair
combed sideways across his skull.
His pudgy forearms shove and pull
as he hauls loaves from the oven
with a long-handled paddle,
and he is powdered all over
with the white weightless dust
that hovers everywhere in the shop,
like angel's breath.

In 1943, the Boy Imagines

that hefty waiters swoop and whirl
among tables of roaring men,
their hands high overhead
swinging two or three bottles
by the neck, or trays slicing
through smoke like river barges
laden with merchandise.
Customers, waiters—
most wear aprons,
full-length and white,
some splattered with axle grease,
others with flour and blood.
All laugh too loudly, faces
red and sweaty, bodies
pink and hairy black
beneath their clothes.
They shout and eat, toast
the stuffy room, yell,
"To life!" and "God is good,"
eyes gleaming, fingers
snatching food from passing trays.
Those eyes know wool and grain,
plate, silver, oil and leather
in the dusty market square,
but know the people who shop there
even better, know the roads
beyond the village and where they lead.

Their cousins cry in the wilderness,
and it flowers. Their uncles
rise suddenly, upsetting tables,
and dance in billowing circles
their vision of the world
that God has promised them.
And *zihr mamas* and *zihr frauen*
scold these drunken boys

or shriek at walls and laundry,
pots on the stove: "This can't
go on! It's not a life!"
They clasp their hands and weep,
then sigh and clean the house once more;
while in doorways on the market square,
squatting on stools, aunts and widows
tear feathers from dead hens
and gasp each time the linen
grazes a tense nipple
inside their clothes.

                This is no country
for those who cringe and cower.
These people understand
any excessive gesture,
any thought or act
that flings the leaping blood
through the body's crooked streets,
anything that grasps and grasps at life.

Shopmen, grandmas, scholars,
laborers, wives, and daughters—
their every flourish and shrug,
their every toothy grin
is done in the sanctity
of God's embrace, as if the air
that encased them and clamped
the woods and fields in place
sat on God's desk
inside a paperweight.
His will was theirs,
and would be done, if they
had the patience to wait for it.

And as the boy imagines this,
his lineage, guided by gun butts,
shuffles through the gates
of Auschwitz and Buchenwald.

GRANDCHILD'S SONGS

One in four, one in four,
1   2   3   4,
one and two, three and four:
which is the recessive gene,
the cloven hoof, the clenching fist,
the secret heart, the dreaming brain?

One and three, two and four,
slide, slide, across the floor.
One of two, of three, of four
takes the suitcase out the door.
Which of them is what I am,
which is what I might have been?

Three and two, four and one:
how much fate and how much luck?
The cloven hoof, the clenching fist,
the secret heart, the dreaming brain —
1 or 2, 3 or 4:
which takes the suitcase out the door?

One and four, two and three:
this one dreamed, and this one wept,
this one stayed, and this one left.
The ones who stayed are dead and gone,
the one in four who made the trip
survived to sing this simple song.

One of four, one of four:
which of them is what I am,
which is what I might have been?

The Poet at Eight

He Rediscovers His Voice

He jumps from the bus when the blond one shoves.
The five boys chase him for blocks—
big shoulders and snatching hands,
all grins and teeth, yelling, "Jew! Jew!"
as he runs from one alley to another
through a section of the city he doesn't know.

Crouching behind crates and garbage cans,
he hears something inside him shout.
The sound rushes from his throat,
breaks open his lips. "Hu! Hu!" it calls.
"Hu, Hu," comes the echo from the brick wall opposite.
And the boy, calmed, no longer alone,
rises and makes his way to the street.

MEETING BENNY LEONARD

"There ain't many who fight back
and vin," his grandfather says. "He's vun who did . . .
So, let me look. Good. Good.
Keep the tie straight, the hair combed."
He stops. "Tell him . . . tell him . . .
I see him fight that Tendler
in nineteen hundred and tventy-vun."

On the bubble-gum boxing card,
he looks small and thin, charging
out of an orange background
in black undershirt and trunks
that resemble a 1920s bathing costume.
"He vuz the greatest lightweight, a real king,"
says the grandfather, reaching
over the boy's shoulder
and tapping the card. "Robinson,
the *shvartzer*, ain't half so good.
He vas quick, had a brain—a brain!"
the old man says and taps his head.
"Not since Samson or Maccabeus
has dhere been such a vun
to show the *goyim* we won't flop dead
like herring at their shoes."

At his best friend Freddie's door:
"Come on. He's just about to leave."
In the living room, he's standing
in a black, stiff-brimmed yachtsman's hat,
so tall in a black suit encrusted with gold
that the boy can't speak.
"Uncle Benny, this is Mort."
A hand swoops from the ceiling
to engulf his own. The black cuff

is ringed with golden bands below a gold star,
his left shoulder swathed in golden braid.
"Hello, kid," he says, and smiles,
standing in the U.S. Navy uniform.

AUNT BERTHA

The massive one marries
a smiling man
who is half her size.
She drives him
from the house each day
and later drives her kids,
as if shaking crumbs
from her apron
out the small apartment door.
Then it's tidy up and clean.
The rooms are spotless,
the furniture never used—
except the kitchen and the beds—
as if the living room
were a museum,
or the burial chamber of a king,
that she's been entrusted to keep.
Is she aunt, mother, wife,
or the caretaker
of some obscure, secret rite?

When the boy is sick
and sent from school,
she gives him enemas,
three or four a day,
feeds him chicken soup
until he thinks he'll burst,
and commands her chubby daughter
to torture him
with cotton swabs on sticks.
This daughter practices
rituals of her own,
probing his hidden paths
with nozzles, thermometers,
and a variety of spoons,

as she experiments
with different methods
to make him scream.

"Mommy, Mommy," he cries,
but Mommy isn't there.
She's vacationing
in Hot Springs or Miami,
and he's been left
in these grim-faced females' care.
By this time, the smiling man
has been driven out
for good, and the aunt's son
has run away to Europe
and the war. The boy
is the only male these females
have to torture now,
and they turn him
slowly in their hands,
poking his ribs to see
if he has fattened up.

Outside, it's Brooklyn,
spring, 1944.
But he is trapped here
in a room with soap operas
and game shows on the radio,
his sole companions
those imprisoned voices
who whisper to him
of war and marriage,
toothpastes and cigarettes,
chewing gums and headache pills.
"Mottle, Mottle,
how we gonna make you well,
you listen to such things?"
It is his aunt.
She fills the doorway

in her faded purple robe,
hands on hips, smelling
of onions and menthol,
and wags her head
like a metronome.
Then she plucks him
from the radio, and bears him
underneath her arm
to the bathroom's
glinting tiles and chrome
for another enema.
Her daughter grins
and pokes his buttocks
when he screams.
"We got to clean you out,
should you still
be full of germs,"
his aunt announces
as she holds him down
but lets him shriek.
Then to her daughter,
or to no one in the room:
"What kind of woman
goes off and leaves a boy . . . ?"
and shakes her head.
Her daughter grins again,
sticks out her tongue,
and pinches him.

By the time his mother comes,
he's well. In the living room
his aunt, triumphant,
stands with feet apart
in the faded robe
and shows him off.
His mother reaches out
a bangled hand
from wild gardenias,

jewels, and furs.
It strokes his cheek.
She nods and thanks her sister
and the pudgy girl,
who hides behind her back,
and gives them
crimson packages
wrapped in yellow bows.
As she accepts,
the aunt is silent,
yet she trembles
like a tree.
The boy looks up.
Her chins are rumbling,
her jaws are clenched,
her mouth is full of words
she will not say.
Tears are welling in her eyes,
and for a moment her hand
clutches his shoulder.
Then, with a grunt,
she shoves him forward.

CAROL

She is the cousin sent
to cart the boy from school
when he is sick; to drag him
screaming through a labyrinth
of streets and subway stops
all the way to Brooklyn
and Aunt Bertha's house,
where she tucks him in bed
and rocks him to sleep,
unexpectedly
murmuring lullabies
as if she were his mother.

Already short and chubby,
with a machine-gun laugh
that balloons her cheeks
and hides her eyes,
she is at the age when girls
tease boys, her giggles
feverish around the edges;
the age when her fingers pinch
although she plans to stroke.

At family gatherings,
she and another cousin
play doctor with the boy
in the abandoned Plymouth
in his grandmother's yard,
determining if his parts
are limber or just limp.
And one Saturday
at the movie show
she clamps his shoulders
with moist palms
so he can't escape

from Karloff carting
bodies in the rain,
while the oozing clay
slips off the shroud,
or comes away in chunks
from the cadaver's
lightning-lit cheeks.
The boy shrieks so loud,
he almost passes out.

Years later, a solid matron
as massive as her mother,
she chides and scolds
her children, shooing them
like a farm wife
shaking her apron
at a yardful of chicks.
One night, eyes moist,
a little tipsy,
she jabs an elbow
in the boy's ribs, and says,
in her Mae West voice,
"You big lug,
you know I love you."
And the boy blinks, realizing
he never doubted it.

PART 3

GRANDFATHER'S CHILD

THE HOLY ONES

Beneath round black brims, around mouth and nose,
the untrimmed beards bristle and sting.
When the mouth inside talks or eats or mumbles prayers,
the whole beard wags like a medieval helmet visor
that hides the head within, that obscures the face
of the one who would not be seen. With lips fluttering holy words,
or in excited squabble; easily startled,
almost girlishly shy—the men who wear these beards
scurry along the street in black overcoats down to their shoes,
as if hurrying to get away, as if trying to vanish
around every corner, always attempting to keep out of sight
or go up in smoke or prayer or cabalistic innuendo.
These are Grandmother's Jews, not Grandfather's.
They are timid, gentle, serene, with smoky eyes
that look out at you as if from another room.

The boy sees them on the street,
talking in clumps of two or three, beards bobbing,
hands flying like doves around their heads.
In the ghetto and the shtetl, their beards and black clothes
are the customary dress of that holy class
who would be close to God. But here,
in midtown Manhattan, at the Diamond Mart,
Jews in double-breasted business suits
stare at them, shake their heads, and then walk on.
When his grandfather sees them, he points and says,
"At getting avay, they vas always good—
at getting avay from they wives vhen they screamed,
from they children vhen they shouted,
at getting avay into books and prayers.
And now in the diamond business
they is getting avay vit murder."
He grins, not angry, really,
and shakes his head in affectionate dismay.

He'd worn a beard himself when he was young,
but that was in another day, and now he looks at these men
as at himself seen from far away.

Bedridden with fever, beyond memory or fear,
the boy sees the face of God rise above his bed,
discharging sparks from His exalted beard.
The face inside that frenzied hair is mild,
a moon to light a small boy's way to sleep
above a snow-slurred land. Both tranquil and wild,
it is a face that befits a towering man
who, in a rage He would regret later on,
condemns His grandchild and all His bickering people
to wander through deserts and ice-capped lands.

THE OTHER HALF

Shadows cover the half of him
he thinks belongs to someone else.
It is not the half
that goes to school by day
and by night obeys his mother,
not the half that leans now
against the old brick wall
in the afternoon sunlight.

It is the half that lounges
slack-muscled in the shade,
the half that his grandfather talks to
about the life in Russia,
and that for the past three days
he's attempted to observe here,
alone, by this alley wall,
on his way home from school.

Nerve ends twitch, muscles flutter.
As yesterday, he clenches his shaded fist,
opens it and pushes down,
shutting his eyes, holding his breath.
Moments later,
when he raises the open hand,
his thumb is cocked like an ear,
and once again
from the joined fingers
the face of a wolf sniffs the air.

DEFENDER OF THE FAITH

Dawdling home from school
late one autumn afternoon,
the boy strays into a street
crowded with garbage cans and shadows.
He is thinking of girls—
the high dark night beneath their skirts
where their legs, like white trees,
disappear. When he looks up,
he is surrounded by boys, big boys,
taller than he by several years.
One stares him in the eye,
bouncing a rubber ball
as pink as a chunk of bubble gum,
and doesn't remove his gaze
each time he snaps the ball
against a pavement square
and it pops back into his palm.

There must be ten of them,
and Columbus Avenue, a sun-splash
down the block, is just too far.
"Catholic or Jew?" the starer says
and flips the ball again.
The boy has encountered this before.
He knows the answer he must give:
it will guarantee safe passage
to that sunny street,
even if they laugh and jeer
and make loud noises at his back.
But he's the grandson of the Wolf,
the one who knocked the Rooski boys
to tears in dusty roads,
and although he is more terrified
than he will ever tell, he knows
that today he will not lie.

"Catholic or Jew?" the other boy repeats.
The answer surges up like muscle
through his chest and arms.
"Jew!" he yells, and the word unfurls
like a pennant from his throat.
He charges the astonished boy
and smashes his head into his chest.
The ball dribbles away. Arms are lassos
around his neck, hands clutch and punch.
He knocks them all aside, lurches on,
flailing and kicking, and all ten boys,
it seems, are now a tent around him
that he is dragging down the street,
until, with a tug, he springs free
and sprints toward the avenue.

Minutes later, he stops for breath,
amazed at what he's done.
Never has his body felt so much his own
yet so much like another's.
Never has he heard it hum
as it does now like trolley wires
in the wind. Thousands of windows
blaze around him like slabs of bronze
on which the Lord is about to write—
those flickering city windows
that will soon go dark one by one.

DOMINOES

The boy loses at every game —
checkers, backgammon, chess.
"Yes! Yes!" the old man roars with every win,
seated on the chair opposite,
and smacks his thighs again and again.
Then the boy discovers dominoes.
He sets his pieces on the table
with the dotted sides towards him.
The markings hover and glow
like an intergalactic Morse code,
whole star systems of white signals.
The old man's squinting eyes
struggle to comprehend,
but all he can see
is a small boy's black wall facing him,
a starless sky — empty, impenetrable,
like the one that surrounds his head.
Each piece the old man places on the table
is a star system of his own, but the boy
matches star clusters, extends galaxies
in unexpected directions,
bewildering the old man,
who watches craftily now
from somewhere behind his eyes
as the constellations spread before him.
The boy claps his hands and yells, "Yes! Yes!"
each time he fits a final piece in place.
And "Yes! Yes!" the old man joins in, "Yes!"
raising his fists above his head
as if now he could hammer nails
into the blackness of the sky.

UNCLE FRANKIE

Then there's the uncle who becomes a cowboy,
the only Jewish cowboy in the West.
Something isn't right, is definitely strange,
even to a nine-year-old living in New York.
Wearing a silver buckle, Stetson hat,
string tie held around his neck by a turquoise ring,
and hand-tooled cowboy boots dyed red and blue and black,
this five-foot, four-inch uncle stomps through Brooklyn,
while everyone mutters and glares at his back.

Arriving at night, he grabs the boy from bed
and whirls him high above his head.
"Sha-prise!" he yells, round-faced and grinning his golden tooth,
more chubby than squat, always returning
from somewhere farther than New Jersey,
somewhere called Utah, Idaho, or Texas,
where, although this is never clear,
he breaks horses for the cavalry.

The week he always allots for his visit
is filled with ice cream and cotton candy every day,
buckskin shirts and gun belts for the boy to keep,
and riding swaybacked horses every night
in Coney Island's Steeple Chase Amusement Park.
The uncle canters around the track, bobbing up and down,
urging his pony to greater speed, while the attendants—
shadowy-faced boys with dirty hands—snicker and smirk.
"You feed dem good? You ain't hittin' dem with no stick—?"
he asks them afterward, and they spit and turn away.
"Hey, you hambrays, look at *mir* when I'm talking at you—"
but they are sweeping up manure or tidying the straw,
and he shrugs and wanders down the midway,
holding the boy's hand in his pudgy palm.

Yes, that's him: buckles and boots and a swaggering smile,
an amiable tough guy so plump and short

he couldn't scare the shyest child.
When he is gone, the boy looks for him
in cowboy films every Saturday matinee—
Gene Autry, Roy Rogers, Johnny MacBrown—
expecting to see him among the cowhands in the posse,
the only one "tugging at the reins of his jittery steed,"
impatient to get going after anything evil,
and to gallop over "dhat dhere" hill
that will take him farther west.
He'll die in a cheap hotel in Denver, of a heart attack,
when the boy is ten, although some cousins
will whisper that he was knifed while he slept.

"But why," the boy asks when he is twenty,
"why did he become a cowboy and go off like that?"
Aunt Bertha sighs, clutches her heart,
and says that as a boy he always loved
to watch the horses in the silent cowboy films.
The others, including his mother, just shrug
and go about their work. By this time
the boy's grandfather is dead and his grandmother
in the nursing home, and only a chance remark
by the boy's mother, when he is forty-four,
sets the matter right, reminding him of what they've all forgotten:
"Your grandfather," she says, "broke horses in the Ukraine
and always kept a horse behind the house—
in Brooklyn yet!" She shakes her head and raises her eyebrows.
But the connection, now, is clear.
And, unwittingly, in any movie where Pugachev,
Yul Brynner, or any cossack chief
gives orders to his mounted men to ride,
the boy searches among those fur-capped warriors
for the one figure jerking his horse this way and that,
the person with the golden tooth and sweaty grin
who doesn't know where he is headed but before the rest
gallops off across the endless steppe
toward that immense, receding blue
that hangs like a theater curtain in the west.

86

THE POET AT TEN

History

Brooklyn, 1946: a tall, sunny morning
near Sheepshead Bay.
Trolley wires drone overhead.
The boy is strolling to the corner candy store,
lingering with each step,
pivoting on his sneakered toes.
On his yellow T-shirt, four heavy medals.
In his right hand, three German coins
given him by a cousin, just returned
from Europe and the war,
whose rough brown uniform
seems woven of tobacco and salt.
The day is full of the same odor of salt,
and the boy is carrying the three coins
to the old man in slippers who owns the candy store,
three coins all the way from Europe
to exchange for chocolate cigarettes,
while something huge, something taller than time,
gathers off the coast,
studded with salt crystals and scratchy wool.

It will remain like that, in his head,
gathering on the horizon, just out of reach:
a flotilla of clouds or icebergs,
which appear but never arrive,
like memories not quite remembered
which push to the edge of his mind.
It will remain like that,
even in the shadowy shop
where the old man in slippers peers at the coins.
Wisps of silk swirl through the room.
They rise from the cigarette
between the old man's fingers,

as he lifts the coins close to his eyes,
then tosses them on the counter
after he shakes his head.
And the counter: it is glass, a gray-black sea.
Candy bars and gum packets hover within,
lying in rows like schools of fish
ready to swim at a word or a touch.

The boy, who knows nothing about history
and follows desires like the odor of warm bread
through streets he cannot remember,
understands that one moment grows into the next
but not that these moments together make up an endless line,
nor that the line pays out to a drowning man
who has grabbed the life ring and holds on,
nor that this man, shrouded in seaweed
that clings like wet tobacco leaves,
can barely make out, through salt-stung lids,
the hull of the rusty freighter bucking through the waves
and towing him forward by this umbilical thread.

To the boy this morning will remain as it is,
every moment plunging like a dolphin
into the sea of each cell.
If he would release this day
with its medals and coins, its sneakers and salt,
if he would let this day whisk over his head
and go down with its clouds behind him,
he would grow older but not wiser,
for the moments would pay out in a line
that would drag a drowned man to shore
without papers or coins,
his face identifying no one the boy knows
yet someone he remembers.

This endless repetition is not obsession—
no matter that the candy store has vanished
and the old man in slippers has disappeared.

Time slows, turns backward, stops,
as the boy shuffles, juxtaposes, reorders
coins, slippers, every tobacco shred—
like timeworn artifacts,
which, if he could detect a pattern
in their seemingly random occurrence,
would disclose the significance of all events.
In time he will learn that he can transform a day
but never change it,
examine events but never explain them.
Yet the act of transformation
will somehow make a difference,
and so he will hoard the moments,
reel them in from that always luminous bay,
as he imagines the curvetting sneakers going,
the laden sneakers coming back;
the vault of that huge morning
with its clouds rolling up;
salt crystals and tobacco shreds;
and, higher than the trolley wires whining overhead,
the medals and coins imprinted against the sky
moments before they flash into the bay.

LEO

The cousin who ran away
to Europe and the war,
an Eisenhower crusader,
returns in 1946,
all five-foot-five of him —
short arms and legs attached
to a six-footer's torso.
He pins medals on the boy,
parades him before his friends,
and sits him on a Packard's hood
so the boy can watch him
scamper for touchdowns
in the Brooklyn streets.

The boundary lines are cars
parked along both curbs —
Plymouths, Fords, De Sotos —
and Leo, emerging
from a flotsam of bodies
which collapses behind him
like an ocean wave,
scoots past the goal line
before the traffic light
can change. "Wahoo!"
"The Tilden tiger's back!"
He canters up the block,
flipping the football
to the others as he trots
past the boy and winks,
grinning at the medals
which celebrate both
his wartime valor
and prewar eminence
in the hundred-yard dash
at city track meets.

Later they visit Debra
at her father's candy store,
a heroine Leo describes
in terms of hills and hollows,
hidden caves and streams.
Weighed down with medals,
the boy advertises
his cousin's triumphs so well,
she accepts Leo's offer
to accompany him
to Loew's Flatbush movie house,
but so shyly, so timidly
that the boy imagines
she has agreed to lead
his cousin to a sacred chapel
on her ancestral lands.

2
Leo is more
a brother
than a cousin,
as much a brother
as a coach.
He takes the boy
to baseball games
at Ebbets Field,
teaches him
the secret code
needed to fill in
the scorecard's
diamond-patterned
centerfold,
and shows him how
to fight and win,
demonstrating
esoteric
combinations
and lethal blows

he swears the boy
to use only
when outnumbered
three to one
or "in event
of certain death."

"Muttel, Muttel,
Muttel Kumputtel,"
he sings to the boy
in a bearish
baritone, then
claps his shoulder,
growls, "Muttel, come,"
and announces that
they'll eat their way
through Brooklyn,
stopping at every
delicatessen
and hot dog stand
from Pitkin Avenue
to Coney Island.
These eating contests
come to an end
when Leo and his friends
pay ten dollars
for a pewter tub
of tutti-frutti
at an ice-cream shop,
hoping the boy
eats every scoop
so they will win
free chocolate sundaes
and banana splits.
The boy can't swallow
a tenth of it,
and they call him

nebbish, schnook,
and Little Lord
Fauntleroy, slap
his head, and spit.

The boy trails Leo
to the houses
of these friends,
listening
to their laughter,
their plans, and,
over the years,
to their crises
with wives and workloads,
cancers and sons,
which pinch the voices
of these men
until they sound
like boys again.

3
With Leo returned, Aunt Bertha's
spotless household is transformed.
Freud's *Interpretation of Dreams*
and books on how to sing and how to calculate
are piled on table and chair,
as if one of them contained the secret
that would open all the windows
hidden in the air and flutter down
mounds of gold dust filtered through the clouds.
With such majesty and power,
Leo could go forth again to conquer continents.
"Knowledge, Muttel, knowledge," he says,
"you've got to learn what life is all about."
But Leo had run from high school to the war
and is forced to take a job as bill collector
for a firm that retrieves sofas and rugs
from those who cannot, or will not, pay.

That lasts until his jaw is broken
and he's thrown down a stairwell in the Bronx.
Next he scorches his fingers and burns both thumbs
altering the face of Brooklyn
by decorating with neon
the darkened shop fronts of Flatbush
in snaky pinks and blues.
Then he changes the skyline of America
by erecting TV antennas,
like secular crosses, on the rooftops
of suburban New York.

4
For the next thirty years
he works for a supermarket chain,
cheering and chiding
the dull-eyed wives of Queens,
who, behind their shopping carts,
smile dreamily at his jokes,
his winks, and his silly songs.
Beginning as butcher, he rises
to manager and then to buyer
for all the stores, marries,
has two daughters, purchases
a condominium in Brooklyn,
and returns from work each night
too tired to eat or talk
or to search for the incantations
hidden in the words of books.

During the eighties,
the supermarket closes down,
and at fifty-nine, he resumes his career
as process server and collector,
which he does without complaint
and not without a certain pride.
He is like those other immigrants—
second generation or first—

farmers in the Midwest and South,
factory workers on either coast,
who are students without schools,
soldiers without armies,
sons grown to fathers,
and citizens controlled by laws,
who one day on the street
find their own eyes in the faces
of the homeless and the poor.

5

All these memories tumble through the dark,
but there is one that returns again and again:
it is Leo kneeling in the street
one afternoon to tie a shoelace.
He is down on one knee, as if getting ready
on the blocks before a race, or praying,
or listening to the count of the referee,
when suddenly his head swings around
and, like an offering on a tray,
he lifts the smile widening on his face
into the traffic and the afternoon sun.

UNCLE DAVE

His six-foot, three-inch frame
is a bleached-out smock of skin
draped around his bones
as he shambles bareheaded
through the neighborhood
in his most valued belonging,
a thick blue overcoat.
"Lis-sen, More-tun.
Af-dher all dhese years,
I still ken feel
dher Roo-shun kalt,"
he drawls and vaguely smiles.
And that's how he is found,
unconscious in the gutter
in his overcoat, robbed
and beaten with a leaded pipe.

They call him Jungle Jim
because, from ten each day
until past twelve at night,
a white pith helmet
rides his bald, hollow-cheeked
Ukrainian head. Hawaiian skirts,
green paper grass in strips,
and football-size coconuts
decorate the walls
of his tiny corner stand
in the Brownsville section
of Brooklyn, where he sells
his famous "Coconut Whip,"
a frothy ice cream
served in paper cups
that he and his wife
make fresh each night
in the room he rents

behind the candy store—
an ice cream so white and smooth
and full of aromatic flavor
you can smell it
halfway down the block.
"Fresh. Look. No
phon-y dhings in here,"
he drawls at anyone who stops,
each syllable floundering
against the heavy tongue
that tolls inside his head.
"So? You vant a cup coconut?"
he asks all those boys and men—
blacks, Puerto Ricans, Irish,
as well as fellow Jews—
who come from everywhere
in Brooklyn on sultry days
to grin at him and taste
the perfumed flavor
of Polynesian seas.
Some come for other things:
"Okay, Tarzan, take it slow
and easy with your hands
and give me all the cash
that's in the candy box."
He is robbed so many times
he gives candy bars to those
who put their guns away
so "no vun vill get hurt."

His grass hut squats
in the middle of shop fronts,
tenements, and traffic,
and he becomes so mild,
so accepting of the world,
that older members of the family
sigh and shake their heads.
Some remember that as a boy

he had been chosen
for the rabbinate
but had to abandon it at twelve
when his father, departing
for America, appointed him
guardian of the family.
And for seven years he had brawled
and defended all of them—
bullied and cursed "the kids,"
cared for his "mama," held at bay
those neighbors and men who came
sniffing around for anything
they could wrestle free—;
and had finally brought them—
sisters, mother, brothers—
past all the crooks who worked
the grimy Baltic ports
safely to the harbor of New York.

Now his teeth are gone,
each come loose and tossed away
like all the years
he never thinks about.
At family gatherings, he sits
with knobby, callused hands
stroking the children's heads,
and stares with smoke-black eyes
at the wall across the room.
Every morning, he wakes up
sore in every muscle.
His mouth aches; he cannot eat.
His six-foot, three-inch frame
is a bleached-out smock of skin
as he shambles bareheaded
through the neighborhood
in his thick blue overcoat.
"Lis-sen, More-tun.

Af-dher all dhese years . . . "
he drawls and vaguely smiles.
And that's how he is found,
unconscious in the gutter . . .

THE OVERCOAT

Every night he dreams of the overcoat in the closet:
navy blue, thick as a carpet, the tips of wool
fading to turquoise, to a feathery peacock.
His uncle had worn that coat every day,
had been mugged in it, had even died in it.
Coat and uncle—they are inseparable in the boy's mind.

Then one night he wakes more shocked than terrified
to find his uncle standing before the bed,
naked, hairy, fish-belly white,
his thin arms clasping his sunken chest,
as if the coal-blue shadow of a bear
no longer shambled from tree to tree
but stood in the headlights skinny and white,
while the overcoat lay behind him
somewhere in the woods, a small black patch
sewn into the fabric of the dark.

UNCLE IKE

Uncle Ike's 1946 De Soto:
the knob of the crooked gearshift shakes
under his hand, or his hand shakes.
This chubby uncle with the tender eyes,
Grandma's baby, first in the family
to be born in the United States
and to earn a college education,
fails at real estate, brokering,
selling cars; and at sixty-five,
his eyes like empty picture frames
that once contained old masters,
he has worked for fifteen years
as an orderly in the county hospital's
mental ward. His wife insists
that everyone call him Bob
because it "sounds American."
Ike, short for Isaac, Abraham's son,
whom God demanded as a sacrifice.

THE WOLF WITHOUT HIS TEETH

"So you caught the wolf without his teeth,"
the old man says, and the grin that follows
is as pink and shy as an infant's smile.
In salmon-colored long johns,
he sits by the side of the bed.
So frail, so shrunk, his cheeks sucked in,
he seems more baffled than surprised,
toeing a slipper toward himself, just as a child
extends his foot to a drifting sailboat in a pond
but can't quite reach, and remains that way—
his leg stuck out, perplexed, wondering what to do next.

From a sunlit glass on the windowsill,
his clenched teeth laugh, daring him
to make the trek across the room.
He blinks and sighs, heaves his weight
onto his feet, and drags himself across.
There, hunched and turned away,
he crams the teeth into his mouth
as if he'd swallow them, stares for a moment
at the clotheslines, tenements, and steeples,
and then turns back with an exaggerated grin.
He's trapped the mocking teeth behind his lips,
and points to them. Now he's straight and tall
and swoops to the boy for a wolfish kiss.
The boy kisses back, and everything seems all right.
But from that day, the boy will taste those teeth
upon his lips—those icy teeth
fresh from the glass in the morning light—
and he will sense that someone else's laugh
is in the old man's face, and that when the old man
turns to him and grins, that stranger's laugh
is being aimed at him.

THE NEW GLASSES

Old and scrawny, his grandfather waits in front of the house.
Two copper-colored mirrors in oval wire frames cover his eyes.
"Prescription," he says, and chuckles at his grandson's face:
he can stare out at the boy, but the boy cannot stare in at him.
"I can look daggers at a neighbor, but vhat can he see?
I can be facing a building, a trolley, a car,
and be rolling my eyes at a *zoftig* voman on the street—
who's to know, who's to guess, who can tell a thing?"
Jauntily he starts upstairs, stops, taps his sunglass frames,
and says, "MacArthur vears dhese vhen he fights the Japanese."

Upstairs, his grandma giggles, points to her eyes,
and says her husband wears a mask "just like some
        cowboy bandit,
or like them boys with pompadours who lean all day on cars,"
and mutters that he is "no longer Jewish."
The old man cackles, lifts his head and howls,
then grabs her and whirls her round. She laughs
and beats her tiny fists against his chest.

The boy sees but is not seen: he is witness to an old man dancing,
a blind old man with copper coins upon his eyes
who gropes from one side of darkness to the other
with a doll-like woman hanging from his neck.
"I got my eye on you, young boychik—you hear?
I see where you are!" the old man calls,
whirling deeper into the shadows with his ancient bride.

THE GRANDMOTHER

She sits and stares at sunbeams
twirling to the kitchen floor
or stars framed by the window square,
until someone enters the room once more.
Then she's up and serving tea
or milk or cakes or Postum
or the glittering chicken soup
that always simmers on the stove.
When everyone has gone, she sighs
and, even if the boy is there,
once more sits and stares
at sunbeams drifting through the air.

And when her eyes close
and she dreams, does she remember
that her life, spent in serving others,
is like the walking stick
that her vigorous wolf-faced man
carried across the world with him
and left here in this empty house?

The sunlight twirls its patterns
to the floor. They drift and roll.
As a girl, she would look at them
and think—think what?
Sometimes when she nods
and smiles and drops her head,
something in her seems to drift
on sunbeams through the room,
and she is dancing in a house
where candles swirl her shadows
all around. The room is buoyant,
it brims with light,
and the shadow that she dances with—
that whirls her in its arms—

her head jumps, her eyes spring wide,
and she is back, seated on the chair
beside the kitchen stove,
a lone traveler in a station
who listens to the metal springs
in the overhead clock.

THE LAST VISIT

"Look who's here," the stout nurse says,
and the old woman turns, shuffles toward him.
He hasn't seen her in a year,
but there's no recrimination in her face.
Expressionless, both eyes filmed and white,
she drags herself toward him—
smaller than he remembers, shapeless
in a pink housecoat, a black hair net
mapping the silver outline of her head.
Her hands come before her,
palms raised like a girl
who would have the moon to praise,
a mother who would hold an infant
high above her hair, or an old woman
who would feel her own cheekbones
in her visiting grandson's face.
She will not touch him,
but outlines his features with her hands,
as if she'd mold a shining from the dark,
a keepsake—medallion or charm—
to carry with her through that night
she faces without resentment or alarm.

Behind her on the bureau
are photographs in cheap gilt frames—
children and children's children
she cannot see, himself among them
squinting in front of blurry trees
and a clapboard house that long ago
was broken into boards and hauled away
from land that is a car lot now.

Her fluttering fingers distract his gaze.
She has remained before him without a word,
shaping his head with her hands.

As if she were molding me of clay,
he thinks, and then remembers
that this was the way,
with a kerchief covering her hair,
she'd bless the candles every sabbath eve
in Brooklyn – or in Vilna: the dusk
fattening to darkness in the dining room,
and she surrounding the candle flame
with both her palms, murmuring
praises to His holy name
and blessings on her children and her house.
The inside of her hands would be bright and warm,
as if draining what little heat she could
from a radiance inside the candle's light.
He's brought a box of chocolates
and photographs of great-grandchildren on a swing,
but he keeps them at his side,
remaining silent within the confines of her hands,
his cheeks flaming with each stroke
as he becomes the torch
that will light her way through an alien land.

All That Is Left

All that is left of his grandmother
resides now in his head:
her white hair tied back in a bun
and her toothless grin,
the gums and inner lips a pinkish-yellow mulch
like the inside of a plum.
Her clothes, her house on Avenue B,
her life in Russia before he was born
vanish before he is twenty-five.

                              Then,
when he is thirty-one,
his mother gives him the wine cups,
two silver cups, like swollen thimbles,
engraved with a hairline sketch of peasant huts
jumbled together by the side of a road.
On one, a polished place
on the tarnished surface shines
like a lighted window.
If he could see inside,
the boy knows he would find
an immaculate goose-down bed;
and on it, laid out
in shimmering metallic pleats,
a radiant white wedding dress.

The Poet at Thirty

The Middle Place

"Learn early, boychik,
and learn it good:
the world's your face.
It's either 'an eye for an eye,
a tooth for a tooth'
or 'turn the other cheek.'
You got to choose and choose right."
The boy finds the world
is a little of both—
a tooth for a cheek,
an eye for a . . . a . . . nose
or an ear— and wonders why
his grandfather
left those features out.
His hair gets pulled and combed,
his lips get kissed and punched,
and no matter how still he sits
or stands behind a door, the world
rushes in. "Sha-prise!"
yells Uncle Frankie
and whirls him in the air.

He's got to make a choice:
is it better to give
than to receive? Receive what?
Pain, of course. Pain's
the issue. Do you
pass it out to the populace
like Joseph bestowing
the stored grain, or do
you absorb it
like a dart board?
"Boychik, boychik."

The old man shakes his head:
"You either a winner
or a loser in this world,
remember that.
There ain't no middle place."
Which years later
is restated as
"Shit or get off the pot,"
by a sergeant from Lubbock.

"Lublin?" asks his grandfather,
leaning out of heaven.

"No, Lubbock. Get back there
where you belong!"

Either-or. Either-or.
The choice is a pendulum
that swings — heavy, razor-edged —
through his brain, fixing his face
in a perpetual grimace.

The months peck at his lips.
The years beat at the bones
in his head, flattening
his features, until that day
when, standing ghastly
before the mirror, he discovers
the impossible middle place,
and in the looking glass of the poem
begins to re-dream his face.

THE MEMORY

The memory opens
like my mother's pocketbook.
And there is it,
behind the lipstick

and the hankies,
that one goodbye
lying on its back
outside of Brooklyn,

staring at the buildings
with bewildered eyes.
Not goodbye dressed
in a kiss or penciled

on an envelope,
but a presence
kicking aside
two hairpins near

my mother's compact,
finding a corner
in which to be forgotten.
Papa, that goodbye

is you, my six years
wearing knickers,
and a taxi ride
down Nevins Street,

sitting on your knees.
The only word you said
was "Son," and I
pushed at your jacket

and off your knees,
shoved years between us,
and lipstick, whisperings,
hairpins and now

children of my own.
I hold them up to you
to ride your knees
as I refused to do,

one old man calling
to another down those
interlocking streets
that vanish behind us.

MOTHER AGAIN

When his mother visits,
she says: "You should lose weight."
And when he does: "You've lost too much."
She says: "The chairs are too low at the table;
they hurt digestion." She tells him:
"Scrub the pot roast before you put it on the stove,"
and "Boil potatoes in their skins
so all the vitamins get cooked in."

"It hurts me so, you live alone," she says,
and has to sigh as loud as a gale every other minute
and beat at the pain he causes in her chest.
She bites her lips, shakes her head,
and every hour releases a hurricane
that almost knocks him off his feet—
all two-hundred pounds of balding professor
with truculent shoulders and gray whiskers on his chin.

She pushes him aside, juggles pots and pans
like a baton twirler at a football game,
this little old woman half his size.
How he stands it, he never knows.
He counts the days until she leaves, allows her
to push him through the house like a long-handled broom,
as she points into corners, rearranges rooms.

He wonders at this man she leads around,
the one he doesn't recognize but lives inside,
directing arms and eyes as if that hair and skin
belonged to some mechanical impersonation of himself—
a golem who performs his master's every wish
and obeys his mother more like a butler
than an obedient son. The question remains
after every visit: Who is he, really?
As for the old woman,

she has no doubt that this other lumbering lout
is her "little boy," and who can argue with a mother?

He soon observes in people's eyes
a recognition of this other self—
acquiescent, slow, a great dumb beast
his closest friends are cautious of,
as if they sense an anger—no, a rage—
growing inside him like a swollen child
that at any moment will rip howling through his skin.
He knows that smothered howling inside is him,
and every time the woman leaves
he slams the walls and bellows like a moose,
as if performing an exorcistic rite
that will shake him from his skin
and allow him to step smooth and steaming
from the birthbag at his feet.

Until then, he nourishes that smothered self—
patient, furtive, a grin inside a mollusk shell.

HEIRLOOMS

Over the years, so many things have been lost or misplaced
or stolen by servants: bracelets and rings, ancestral gold;
his great-grandmother's pearls, given by an uncle in Krakow,
strung in Vienna, and fished from a Polynesian lagoon;
a sword taken from Syria during the Third Crusade,
belonging to a duke who had sold his estate
to a great-great-uncle in textiles in Prague.
Its blade, engraved all over with flowers and vines,
resembles a tattooed man hiding at the forest's edge,
watching men in armor disembarking on his shores.
Brass candlesticks, bangles, silver-encrusted combs . . . .

But to find the oval brooch—three ruby blossoms
joined in a bouquet by a leaf-like golden bow—
to come upon it unexpectedly in a display of pocket watches,
stickpins, and semiprecious stones—is to experience a shock
that makes him start and catches the breath in his throat.
This brooch looks like the perfect replica of one—
made in Paris and bought in a fashionable shop in Minsk—
that his great-grandfather gave his wife in 1986,
on the thirtieth anniversary of their wedding day,
and that he often played with as a boy in his uncle's Brooklyn home.

Now it glitters up at him from the rickety card table
owned by a retired electrician with a hearing aid,
who tells him, "My daddy was a sharecropper from Kentucky
and my daddy's daddy and all them before that
came from Ireland's emerald sod,"
as he motions somewhere behind him with a can of beer,
somewhere behind the Sunday flea market at the drive-in theater
in a small town on the northern coast of California.

THE POET AT FORTY

The Four Freedoms

If the first bondage
was you, Mother,
then the first freedom
was my birth.

You were the statue
in the harbor: there,
but so remote. When
I knocked on you,
you clanged, hollow,
and never answered,
never called my name.
I clambered up
the wooden steps
high inside you,
dizzy and breathless
from all those turnings,
the air so stale and close
with trapped sunlight
and dead moth wings
I sagged and groaned,
forgetting why
I'd come, finding
at the top only
the skyline there
across the river,
as if that had been
my destination
all along,
not realizing
until years later
that there had been
no reason

for my pilgrimage,
that the journey
was the journey
and nothing more.
There on your island,
everyone passing by,
you were meant to be seen,
meant to be the meaning
anyone wanted you to be,
and that knowledge,
not the torch you held aloft,
was my second freedom.

I ran into the heartland,
Lady, as far from you
as distance would allow,
tore at my clothes and eyes,
heaped my head with dust.
But when I scooped
bright mirrors
from the rivers, I saw
that my hair *was* dust
and that your features
were reflected in my own.
And this recognition
was my third freedom.

The fourth freedom is *this*—
these words that like a hand
reach toward you, seeking
to touch, hold fast,
before they must let go—
these words I cultivate
which can transform
a continent
into a garden
or a wilderness,
change the universe

into an endless ballroom
lit with chandeliers
or a shining bracelet
of chromosomes
where this family
of microbes, plants,
and animals – creatures with
and without wings –
dance on, pulsing
through starlight
and cell light,
through atom light
and dream light
in sparks that wink on and off
like a maze of fireflies
whose haphazard design
gives shape to the hollow dark.

Part 4

It Begins Right Here

It Begins Right Here

1

My grandfather drops
the lighted cigarette
in the muddy wheel rut
outside his house the day
he decides to leave Russia.
I had forgotten this,
although it has been told me
countless times by my mother,
the six-year-old watching
from the kitchen window.
"He is looking west,"
she says, "towards Vilna.
I see it clear as yesterday."
It begins here, and I
will not forget it again.
What the old man chooses—
dropping the cigarette,
kicking at clods with muddy boots—
is what I will become.

He harnessed the horse cart,
tumbled in baggage, crockery,
sons, daughters, wife,
sweat and garlic sliding
beneath his undershirt
and holy prayer shawl,
his rancid sheepskin coat
billowing like wings;
and he clopped past hamlets,
villages, towns, and cities;
past continents and oceans;
past storage tanks, tool works,
corner diners after dark;
past cancers, wars,

no bread in the cupboard,
roaches, tetanus,
children leaving home—
clopped past everything
to where I sit now
in this house above the bay
where the green Pacific
emerges from the fog.

My grandfather has been dead
for more than fifty years.
He died without knowing
where California was.
But sometimes I think he comes
to the door and with cap in hand
stands outside with sightless eyes.
At such times, I'm convinced
that his eyes are in my head,
and that for both of us,
and for my mother, whose vision
is diminishing to memories
in a city on another shore—
it begins again right here.

2

In the mountains above the bay,
both my daughters murmur in sleep.
Moonlight is sailing through the window.
Their mouths are open as they dream.
I don't know if they dream of Russia
or of the tenements of New York
or of the continent that ends here,
the water's beaten silver
slipping outward from the shore.
The mountains breathe around them:
honeysuckle, mustard, clover,
lilac, rhododendron, mint,
and the musty leaf pack

on the shadowy forest floors—
redwood, pine, and bay.
All these scents stream skyward,
and with them, like voices in a choir,
rise my daughters' dreaming breath.

For both my children adrift in sleep,
for whatever lives in them of me,
the dream begins right here.

3
With a friend, I wandered out
to watch the evening sun.
He had a special place in mind
and led me to a cliff above the bay
where cypress held a rusty light
and gray pines swayed.
"There," he said and pointed
to a black cloud
wheeling low above the sea.
The water was flat and polished pink,
dark hollows shifting here and there
like changing currents in a dream.
"See?" The cloud was spinning
like a wheel of ash,
and I saw it was composed
of sharp-winged birds,
thousands of sooty shearwaters
skimming the surface of the bay,
feet and wing-flick ruffling up a froth
or detonating the surface when they dived,
until hundreds wrestled with the water,
snapping beaks and fanning wings
beating up a storm of waves and surf
as others fell like a blizzard,
crashing through to "Fish! Fish!
There must be millions of them!
What a feed!" he said and looked away.

There was a stain beneath the water,
a school of anchovies
three hundred yards long,
sprawling this way and that
beneath the clamoring birds,
whose shadow hugged the stain so closely
that an image fluttered through my head
of the bay lying open
for thousands of years beneath the sun
like an old chipped serving bowl
where the feeders were no different
than the food on which they fed.

Next year on the wharf,
I was leaning against a rail
just as the fog burned off,
and it began:
                a rustle,
static across a widening gulf,
a cloud low and far away
but as it approached
whipping up small peaks
and racing above what seemed
its shadow on the bay,
until I was engulfed:
starchy wings and battered surf,
beaks chopping water
and shredding it to froth
as they snatched at fish.
I was spattered and stained.
I couldn't breathe. Below me
were eyes, acres of eyes,
eyes smeared with an oily light,
edged in sediment, in winy mud;
everywhere eyes streaming by,
thousands of silvery disks
with black holes in their centers
like mine shafts hurtling

to the end of the universe;
eyes that neither beseeched
nor accused, but watched
from the outskirts of the present
as they sank into the past.
And the bay, suddenly,
in a tinfoil shift of wind,
was a sky full of drowned stars.

For me, each day begins
right here.

4
                    Teeth have been found,
human teeth, in the tidal mud,
and flints, hand axes, arrowheads,
burial grounds in the hills.
The words *aptos* and *soquel.*
Not much else. The Indians
followed their eyes beyond the sun.
Their irises flashed for a moment,
and then they were done.
The grandees and conquistadors,
the padres in rough robes,
have shriveled with their land grants
beneath adobe walls.
They spice the earth around us.
They are smoke or wind or waves.
They are leaves that tongue the breeze
like tiny bells, chimes
that are felt as well as heard,
like bee stings beneath the skin,
endings in which, each moment,
all things once more begin.

5

A student, grinning,
shows me an old photograph
of his Italian grandfather.
And I think, *My grandfather*
must have looked like that.
Surrounded by family, braced
against the backrest of the chair,
big-knuckled hands gripping the arms
as if he were about to spring,
the old man glares at me.
There's arrogance in those eyes,
defiance in that out-thrust chin;
and the usual costume
to accompany the pose:
handlebar mustache,
high stiff collar,
silver watch chain
across a black wool vest.
The print is muddy brown.
It could be Sicily
or Spain or even Russia,
but it's not. Outside
the photograph, it's Monterey.
A muddy daylight shifts
across a muddy bay:
                    Sardines,
silver-sided shoals of them,
pack the waters.
Canning factories
clatter and shake and steam.
Discarded fish heads and fins.
Scalding fish oil
that leaves a greasy film
on every townsman's skin.
Twenty-five tons
were canned every day.
This old man knew Ferrante;

used the zigzag lightning
of his lampara net;
was one of the colony
of Sicilian fishermen
that Ferrante, like Moses,
led to this fog-swabbed bay
and to whom Ferrante said, "Here.
You have been promised this."
For thirty years, the old man
fished and overfished the bay.
Then it was done. Arrogance
and promises were not enough.
For sardines and fishermen,
it ended where it had begun.

6
The fog removes a hill
beyond my neighbor's fence.
Out of sight behind the house,
the road and redwood grove
have been missing for a week.
And there, across the bay,
the entire mountain range
has vanished overnight
to be replaced by nothing
but a gap of ragged gray.
It is the fog, then—the fog
that makes the countryside
a landscape we invent,
a jigsaw-puzzle scene
where pieces are always missing
or constantly rearranged,
exposing absences
that take us unaware,
gaps our minds must fill
with landmarks we remember
or places we invent.
Now and then, the land

shifts beneath my feet,
the house around me trembles.
There can be fog outside or sun,
but at such moments I think
the landscape and the elements
contrive to make us dream.

Downtown, last month, near
a women's clothing shop,
a girl in beaded buckskins,
hair braided like a squaw's,
padded up beside me, and stared
through the plate-glass window
at the gold glitter pumps
and genie pants on display.
She was eighteen or so
and white as a picket fence
and could have been the sister
of the boy across the street
who sat cross-legged on a bench
in beard and hemp-tied robe,
as if he were Jesus begging
in front of the five-and-ten.
I see them everywhere:
carrying blankets and guitars
to somewhere else, dressed
like apparitions in a dream,
or like foreigners, or like the dead.
When he was young, my grandfather
must have looked like them.
What he was looking for,
they look for now. No,
it isn't quite the same.
But who am I to talk,
who have lugged an old man's dreams,
and the dreams of the old woman
who was once his daughter,
across a continent

to resurrect them here
above a foggy shore?

Who are these children,
these actors without a play,
these masquerading bands
who traipse past cairns and graves
and all the unmarked places
in a shifting countryside
where dead men's dreams
are flowering around us
in trees and rocks and weeds,
where the stares of birds and fish
remind us of the eyes
of that vague, fog-laden form
who shambles from our sleep
and whom we almost recognize?

More and more I think
that if I looked closely
at the tapering face bones
of that buckskinned white girl,
I would find a daughter.
Weren't those our skeletons,
costumed in their separate skins,
who wandered here, hauling
our parents' crockery and clothes
to this fogbound place?
And aren't these children
the ones we dreamt about
who have tumbled onto a landscape
more authentic than the one
on which our imaginations
could put down houses?
Our dreams like fog
swirled around them
and clung, clung to these children,
these muscles of our eyes,

these skins of our breath,
whose only hope now—
and our own—is to feel
the trembling beneath their feet
and recognize
that the land is as unsure
as they are, and as young.